EDDIE GREEN

The Rise of an Early 1900s Black American Entertainment Pioneer

By Elva Diane Green

Published in the USA by:
BearManor Media
P O Box 71426
Albany, Georgia 31708
www.bearmanormedia.com

Printed in the United States of America
ISBN   978-1-59393-966-3 (paperback)

Book & cover design and layout by Darlene Swanson • www.van-garde.com

Dedication

This book is dedicated to my grandson,
Edward Nathaniel Green, to present to him
an example of what can be accomplished
regardless of obstacles, as demonstrated
by his great-grandfather, Eddie Green.

Contents

Introduction

Few people remember Eddie Green today, despite the fact that he was a star on the stage, on radio, on early television, and in some movies. Some may remember Eddie from his popular 1940s radio roles as "Stonewall, the lawyer in *Amos 'n' Andy*, or as "Eddie, the Waiter" in *Duffy's Tavern*, in which he appeared from 1941 to 1950. Some, in the field of songwriting, may remember that Eddie wrote the extremely popular song, "A Good Man Is Hard to Find," which was recorded by such greats as Sophie Tucker, Billie Holiday, and Frank Sinatra.

Even less well-known today is that Eddie co-starred with Bill "Bojangles" Robinson in the Mike Todd presentation, *Hot Mikado*, as Koko, the High Court Executioner, in 1939, or that Eddie appeared on the first public demonstration of television, which was broadcast from New York in 1936, or that Eddie made five all-Black cast movies, which he directed, produced, and starred in, from his two movie studios, Sepia Art Pictures Company and Sepia Productions, Inc.

At the time of the above mentioned projects, Eddie was quite well-known. From the writing of "A Good Man is Hard to Find" in 1917 until his death in 1950, Eddie became famous. Newspaper columnists made sure his name was constantly in the news. They reported on his restaurant openings, his Broadway successes, his radio appearances. They even reported on his favorite foods—greens and ham hocks—but that was then.

This book is my attempt to bring my father's name back to the fore of the public's memory, both as a way to honor his vast amount of work, and as a way to provide an example of what a person can accomplish in life regardless of certain obstacles, and despite, or maybe because of, a less than desirable background.

My first source of information about Eddie, was, of course, my mother, Norma. Eddie was starring in the *Duffy's Tavern* radio program as "Eddie, the waiter," and had just wrapped up an appearance in the Paramount movie, *Ed Gardner's Duffy's Tavern* (1945), when they married. Over the five years that they were married, Norma learned a few of the basics of Eddie's life, such as, where he was born and how he ran away from home at the age of nine. She learned of a few of the highlights, like the first song he wrote, and the fact that he sang "Titwillow" on Broadway in *Hot Mikado* (1939), and that he had once been mentioned in a Walter Winchell column. However, the information that my mother passed on to me was minute, compared to what I have uncovered over the past five years since her death. Therefore, this book's focus is on Eddie's life, as I have come to know it, through perusing documents in libraries and museums, by searching the World Wide Web, and by listening to numerous tapes of Old Time Radio.

In 1996, while browsing in the Los Angeles Central Library, my mom found a picture of Eddie performing at the mike with the cast of the *Amos 'n' Andy* radio show. That picture gave impetus to this book-writing venture. As a matter of fact, that picture was the only other picture I had of my father until I started researching Eddie's life. A house fire destroyed a large part of my mother's personal photos and left her with just one studio head shot of Eddie. I have since acquired many pictures of Eddie from museums, libraries, posters, and newspapers.

In 1997, my mom and I were making plans to collaborate on the writing of this book, when she was diagnosed with breast cancer. The doctors caught it in time, with weeks of chemotherapy and radiation. In 1998, a devastating, unexpected death occurred in our family. This book was placed on a shelf.

I decided to become a Psychology Major, and I began attending the local Community College. I was working and helping out as a baby-sitting grandmother to a teenager, so I was pretty busy. By 2006, I no longer had a job and was working sporadically on the putting-together of the book, when mom's cancer returned. Over the next few years, our family pulled together to help my mom and her third husband through their illnesses. My mother died in October 2010 at the age of eighty-seven. Though she was not able to witness the completion of this book, she was a large part of the beginning.

Thankfully, Eddie was very much the entertainer and business man. Ninety-five percent of his life was entertainment, and that includes the business part of his life. From the time he wrote his first song until his last performance, Eddie Green's name was in the newspapers.

Acknowledgments

Before I began this book, I visited the African-American Museum at Exposition Park in Los Angeles to see an exhibit of 1940s African-American entertainers. I hoped to find information about Eddie, which I did. Most amazing to me, however, is that I also found my mother hanging on the wall in a picture with Eddie at a USO club. I was flabbergasted. I returned later to find out how I could get a copy of that picture. The gentleman that I wound up speaking with, a Mr. Rick Moss, was extremely helpful, and although he could not find that particular picture, he did help me find others. This was the beginning of a fruitful search for photos that are in this book, and I would like to thank Mr. Moss for his help. I would also like to thank the staff at the Natural History Museum of Los Angeles at Exposition Park, for helping me locate old addresses. The staff at the Los Angeles Central Public Library were very patient with me, as I required a lot of help browsing their card catalogues, and understanding their cumulative copyright books. I want to thank the staff at the Los Angeles Family History Library (now known as Family Search Library). They provided me with exactly what I needed at the time, access to computers and photocopying equipment, maps, and one-on-one genealogical help. I thank the staff at The Margaret Herrick Library for their diligence, where I found information I didn't even know existed. Thank you, Mr. Linden Anderson of the Schomburg Center for Research in Black Culture, for assisting me with the photo ordering process. I also want to thank, Mr. Lloyd Clayton and the employees of the Mayme Clayton Museum, and the employees of the Wisconsin Historical Society. Mr. E. Gains, of the *New Pittsburgh Courier*, provided invaluable assistance in locating photos, despite his busy schedule. I want to thank Ron, from the Vitaphone project for his help and Mike Bennett, of Peel the Paint, for the great painting of my father, and for the taped programs. Thank you to Mr. and Mrs. Hank Hinkell for the Jubilee CD's, and thank you to Scott Scroggins for his help in locating Eddie's music. A big thank you to Mr. Martin Grams, Jr., the author of, *Duffy's Tavern - A History of Ed Gardner's Radio Program*, for all his help and encouragement and for paving the way, by gathering a vast amount of information about Old Time Radio programs and, also, for introducing me to the folks at The Society to Preserve and Encourage Radio Drama Variety and Comedy, Inc. (SPERDVAC). I would like to thank John and Larry Gassman from SPERDVAC for honoring me with an interview on their internet radio program. Thank you to Mr. Ed Gardner, Jr., for our communications, and for granting me the use of his pictures from our fathers' days on the *Duffy's Tavern* radio program. I thank Jerry Haendigis, and J. David Goldin for their efforts in gathering and publishing up-to-date information. Thank you, also, to Mr. Grey Smith of the Heritage Auction Gallery, for your assistance in helping me acquire images of the *Comes Midnight*, and the *Mr. Adam's Bomb* posters. Thank you to Mr. Tom Meyers, Executive Director, Fort Lee Commission, and Richard Koszarski, Fort Lee Commission member, and Rob Ford for your attention to my e-mails. Thank you Mr. Davenport, of the Angeles Funeral Home, in Los Angeles, California, for your help in regard to the Hill family photograph. A great big thank you to Mr. Jerry Geltzer, for making himself available to me, and providing me with his vast knowledge of the legalities of the movie business, his knowledge of the book-writing business, and the "race" movie industry, and his willingness to be of service. I must thank the following people who were of immense help in proofreading this book: Mary Carey Crawford, Ian Dickerson, Steve Rogers, S. Robinson (you know who you are), Larry Groebe, Robert Young (Sandy), John Coupal, Joe Tobin, Stan Delahoyde, Peter Genovese, Andrew Steinberg, Ian

Grieve, and my sister-in-law, Jackie Lewis. I would like to thank my blogger friends for hanging in there with me, you were and are a major part of this quest. Thank you Sharon Cooper, for finding me. Finally, thank you so much to my family, Norma, my mother, Melony, my daughter, Edward, my grandson, my brothers and sister, Lance, Brad, Brian, and Donna, and the in-laws and nieces and nephews and cousins who cheered me on, providing me with the impetus needed to complete this book.

Chapter One

Baltimore, Maryland

Edward (Eddie) Green was born in 1891, to William and Janie Green (nee' Nichols). The Greens lived in the poverty stricken neighborhood of East Baltimore. Eddie's mother took in washing, and Eddie's father may have worked on the docks. As a child, Eddie hated the surroundings in which he lived. He hated the dilapidated alley house that he lived in, and he hated the neighborhood. In 1891, Blacks and poor Whites were relegated to living only in East Baltimore, and in 1891, East Baltimore was a slum. People lived in ramshackle wooden, or tin one-room houses, with no plumbing, as there was no sewage system. Leukemia was rampant. There were open drains, lots filled with weeds, and garbage was allowed to accumulate in the alleyways. At nine years of age, Eddie left home to fend for himself.

The information I have on Eddie's education is conflicting. Eddie told my mother that he taught himself to read by picking up newspapers from the street. However, in later census documents, it is noted that he finished two years of high school. It is possible that Eddie went to school as he got older. However, after Eddie left home, school was not a priority for the nine-year-old. He had to actually provide for himself. Eddie became interested in reading magic books and became so proficient in the art that he began touting himself as the "Boy Magician," visiting various churches and halls in Baltimore, offering to perform. I can only assume that Eddie was compensated with food or a place to stay, in lieu of money, as he was too young to earn a wage.

During those years, there were family members who contributed to Eddie's welfare. In a 1939 Baltimore article, Eddie said, "When he returns now it is only to see the city, for all the older members of his family have passed on." He said, "This included Bishop and Mrs. J. A. Handy." Bishop J. A. Handy, at one time, was well-known throughout the country for his religious and civic work with the AME church, and his wife Mrs. J. A. Handy, was the former Mary Nichols Frisby, possibly Janie Nichols' sister. Meaning Mrs. Handy may have been Eddie's aunt.

Bishop Handy wrote in an article, in 1902, "I was born in Baltimore, Maryland, Friday, December 22, 1826. I am the first son of Ishmael and Nancy Handy. My father was a slave and my mother was free. I was licensed as a local preacher by the late John M. Brown, in August, 1860, while he was pastor of Bethel A.M.E. Church, Baltimore. In 1892, I was elected, in company with Benjamin F. Lee and Moses B. Salter, one of the Bishops of the African Methodist Episcopal Church." Bishop Handy passed on in 1911.

Mrs. J. A. Handy, Mary, was born in 1848, to John and Mathilda Nichols. After her mother died, Mary left her home in Baltimore at age seventeen, moving to Philadelphia, where in 1876, she married Mr. S. Clark Frisby. After six-and-a-half years, Mr. Frisby died, and after a four-year span of widowhood, in 1886, Mary became the wife of the then Presiding Elder, James A. Handy.

Mrs. Mary F. Handy became well-known in her own right, for her religious and civic beneficial work, after marrying Bishop Handy. She became the President of the Parent Mite Missionary Women's Society, which she organized in 1907 (now The Women's Missionary Society of the A.M.E. church). In her later years, Mary F. Handy became President Emeritus, and the Matron of the Bethel Old Folks Home. Mary F. Handy passed on in 1932.

The current Handy Simmons Scholarship Commission was established by the Women's Missionary Society to honor the memory of, and service rendered by, Mary F. Handy, and Sandy G. Simmons, the first President of The Women's Home and Foreign Missions.

Between 1900, when Eddie left home, and 1908 or 1909, when Eddie married for the first time, Bishop Handy and his wife Mary, had provided some type of family life for Eddie. To my knowledge, Eddie did not discuss these matters with my mother, other than to tell her about his dislike of his early home life.

In 1904, there was a devastating fire in Baltimore that destroyed seventy-three city blocks and needed more than 1,231 firefighters to bring the fire under control. The fire burned over thirty hours and destroyed over 1,000 buildings. The cost of the damage amounted to $125 million. Eddie would have been thirteen years old, maybe living on his own, or maybe he found refuge with Bishop and Mrs. Handy. However, Eddie seemed to come out unscathed.

In about 1907, Eddie began renting halls and hiring assistants to help with his magic acts. He must have done well, because in 1909 at the age of eighteen, Eddie married for the first time. Julia Roles was eighteen years old and a native of Baltimore, where they were married on June 20, 1909. A year later, Eddie and Julia became parents of a little girl whom they named Hilda. I believe that Eddie had also begun working as a laborer, as I found a listing for him in Polk's Colored Directory as a laborer. Within the next five or so years, Eddie would find an entertainment venue in which he could work as both a performer and a sometime handyman.

Chapter Two
A Good Man Is Hard To Find

In 1916, while continuing to perform as a magician, Eddie wrote a silent movie titled, *Eddie Green's Rehearsal*, which gives an early indication of the direction in which he was heading. This movie was directed, produced, and distributed by him, and he was the entire cast. The movie was about a man by the same name of Eddie Green, who is desperate to get into show business. Eddie borrows a friend's clothes and car, and goes to an audition. He tells jokes, sings, and generally performs to an encore. This scenario proved to be prophetic.

The movie did not actually make it to the big screen, at least not in its original format, and not until 1939, but it had enough merit to warrant a mention, in a 1998 book titled *African American Film Through 1959* by Larry Richards.

In April of 1917, the United States entered World War I. Eddie was twenty-six years old when he reported to his draft board. The information on his registration card provided me with his address at the time: 1405 Ten Pin Alley, in Baltimore. Ten Pin Alley was literally an alley, located in what was then Ward 5, a part of East Baltimore, which, though poor and crowded, was basically the only place poor Blacks were allowed to live. Also noted on the card was his occupation as an actor, his place of employment—the Standard Theatre in Philadelphia, and the fact that he had a wife and child.

In regard to Eddie's first daughter Hilda, I only met her once in 1950. I have since discovered that she passed on in 1989.

The Standard Theater was owned by a Mr. John T. Gibson, a native of Baltimore, who also ran Gibson's Auditorium Theatre on South Street and made good money booking Black Vaudeville acts on the national "chitlin circuit." Stars such as Bessie Smith and Ethel Waters, also performed at the Standard Theater. Ticket sales at the Standard helped make Gibson the "richest Black man in Philadelphia."

While at the Standard Theater, Eddie dropped the magic tricks from his act. After catching one of his shows, a stage manager told Eddie to "Get rid of the paraphernalia and just do comedy; you are really funny." Eddie took the man's advice and began performing as a comedian, eventually adding singing and dancing to his routine.

During this time, Eddie wrote his first song, "A Good Man is Hard to Find," which he copyrighted on December 28, 1917, in Chicago. "A Good Man is Hard to Find" is a bluesy type of song, explaining what a woman should do when she manages to get a "good" man. Six months later, Eddie sold his song, and on June 2, 1918, the song was copyrighted by Pace and Handy Music Publishers (Home of the Blues), and the song went on sale as a piano roll in the *Fort Wayne Gazette.*

"A Good Man is Hard to Find" became a hit. January 4, 1919, Eddie got his first top billing as an entertainer, though his name as the songwriter was in tiny print. The name of the song was in big, bold letters right at the top of *The Billboard* page. *The Billboard* listed the song as "a 1,000,000 copy hit, sure fire applause getter for any singing act or combination on the stage."

Marion Harris, a popular singer, most successful in the 1920s, the first widely-known White singer to sing jazz and blues songs, recorded the song in 1919 for Victor Records. [Her recording has been digitized at the Library of Congress Packard Campus for Audio Visual Conservation.]

In 1919, Eddie put together a company of eighteen players that he called the "Deluxe Players," and as owner and manager of the "Deluxe Players," he began to tour the South, featuring "A Good Man is Hard to Find," performing in places such as Tampa, Florida and St. Louis, Missouri. Eddie and his company were a sensation in St. Louis at the Booker Washington Theater, as was printed by the *St. Louis Argus*, January 9, 1920: "Green with his droll humor, and his coterie of performers made a big hit during a previous performance at this house." The show bristled with tuneful melodies, graceful and eccentric dances, and a barrel of side-splitting comedy."

"A Good Man is Hard to Find" caught the attention of Miss Sophie Tucker. She began her theater career in 1907. One of her first professional jobs was working as a singer in blackface—meaning that she covered her face and hands with black cork in order to look like a Negro—and she was billed as the "World-renowned Coon Shouter" on Joe Wood's small-time circuit. She was forced to wear blackface on stage to detract from her large size and what her producers thought was her "ugly" face. She hated blackface because it seemed to serve as a mask between her and the audience, and

Sophie Tucker Says (1919) *Dramatic Mirror.*]

after having her make-up kit stolen one night, she decided to go on stage without "blacking up." She became a hit by using self-parody in regard to her large size and racy comedy. By 1919, ragtime and blues were all the rage, and Black-written blues and jazz songs became her specialty. While later performing in the Sophie Tucker Room in Reisenweber's in New York, she sang "A Good Man is Hard to Find" every night for ten consecutive weeks, and "will continue to use it until her engagement terminates." Miss Tucker said that "A Good Man is Hard to Find" is "the best blue number she has ever used." She became one of the most popular entertainers at that time, who was also known as "the last of the red hot mammas."

"A Good Man is Hard to Find" has since been recorded as a blues number, a fox trot and a swing number, by such greats as Wilbur C. Sweatman's Jazz Orchestra, Les Brown and his Orchestra, Louis Prima and his Orchestra, Jess Stacy and his Orchestra, Dorothy Loudon with the Honky Tonks, William's Cotton Club Orchestra, Muggsy Spanier, the Alabama Red Peppers, "Fats" Waller, Bessie Smith, Frank Sinatra, Rosemary Clooney, Cass Daley, Big Maybelle, Brenda Lee, Nancy Wilson, and Carol Channing, to name a few, and a version of the song has been heard in Woody Allen's recent film, *Blue Jasmine* (2013), and even more recently in HBO's 2015 presentation of *Bessie*. As was Sophie Tucker before her, Bessie Smith was instrumental in popularizing "A Good Man Is Hard to Find."

As the years went by, Eddie must have been aware of the impact this song had on people. At the time he wrote this song, though, he probably needed the money he received when he sold it to Pace and Handy. The popularity of this song announced his arrival, and with his talent for getting laughs, and his willingness to work for what he wanted, Eddie was on his way up.

Chapter Three

The Columbia Circuit

In a 1937 interview with the *Milwaukee Journal*, Eddie recounted a story of an experience that helped him get into the theater in New York. After leaving St. Louis, and while performing in Tampa, Florida, he noticed an advertisement in the newspaper for a comedian. He wired the manager from Tampa, after having an engraver make him a letterhead that looked "like a million dollars." At the top of the wire, it read in large letters, "Deluxe Players." The next line read, "Eddie Green, owner, comedian-manager-director-organizer." Eddie added fancy frills around the edges. The New York manager, impressed, offered him the job. I believe the job for which he was hired was as a comedian in Barney Gerard's *Girls De Looks*, because I found an ad from July 23, 1919, sending out a call for auditions and rehearsals at the Yorkville Casino, for three shows, one of them being *Girls De Looks*, which was the show in which Eddie had his first performance in 1920. Further on in this article, after being questioned on his philosophy of show business, Eddie was quoted as saying "If you've got the talent, you can't miss in the long run, even if it's mighty long!"

Eddie was multitasking before this was a social term. While preparing for his spot with Barney Gerard, he wrote three more songs, "Don't Let No One Man Worry Your Mind," "You Can't Keep a Good Girl Down," and "Valley of Wonderful Years." This last song was a collaboration with L. Sears, who wrote the words, while Eddie wrote the melody.

At the time, Sophie Tucker was appearing in a play titled, "*Hello Alexander*," in which she sang "Don't Let No One Man Worry Your Mind," which received notice in *The Billboard* giving credit to Eddie Green, writer of "A Good Man is Hard to Find."

In March, Eddie also collaborated with musical comedy writer Billy McLaurin, and wrote the words and music for the song, "Blind Man's Blues." "Blind Man's Blues" would go on to be recorded by Sara Martin and the Clarence Williams Blue Five, on the Okeh record label.

Eddie began performing in *Girls De Looks* (1920), a Barney Gerard Burlesque show that featured beautiful girls and some of the cleaner comedy. The principles of the play, Joseph Watson and Will Cohan, portrayed two aspiring stock brokers, the former being the wise one of the two, and the latter being the happy-go-lucky one, whose efforts to get rich quick lead them in a series of funny situations, which, according to the newspapers, provided the audience with loads of laughs.

Barney Gerard was a prolific screenwriter and producer of both plays and film. He was born on June 12, 1870 in New York City, and he and Eddie formed a good working relationship that lasted for a few years. Mr. Gerard died June 30, 1962, at age ninety-two. Joseph K. Watson, was a Vaudevillian and comedian, who also wrote material for Al Jolson, and his partner, Will Cohan, was also a comedian.

As a comedian with *Girls De Looks*, Eddie began touring the Columbia Circuit, where he became known as "Simp." On December 29, 1920, the *New York Clipper* printed this assessment of his performance: Eddie "Simp" as porter and bellhop, did well. In the ship scene, Simp put over a corking good dance specialty."

Around this same time, there was a husband and wife act performing in Vaudeville, the husband's name was also Eddie Green. This Eddie Green, however, was performing with a different circuit, and so, Eddie placed an ad in the local paper that stated in part, "Eddie Green wishes his friends to know, in order that he may not be confused with another of that name who is working over at the T. O. B. A. Circuit, that he is working with the *Girls De Looks* on the Columbia Burlesque wheel." [Theater Owners Booking Association was the Vaudeville circuit for Black performers in the 1920s.]

Eddie, now twenty-nine years old, was on the road with his first Burlesque show. His climb had begun. He had left his "Deluxe Players" behind and begun to put his energies into his performances on the Columbia Circuit.

Eddie had more than likely grown use to traveling and having to be away from his family, as he had first started commuting in 1917 from Baltimore. We can only wonder how his wife felt about his absences.

In December 1920, Eddie wrote a letter to *The Billboard*, in which the editor of the newspaper said, "The following letter from Eddie (Simp) Green, who is with Barney Gerard's *Girls De Looks* Burlesque show, is beyond doubt the most unselfish communication that has come to us since the department has been started."

The letter read: "Jack, just a note to tell you that the boys playing this town find it so hard to get rooms, that I think it would benefit all of them greatly if you would say in your notes, that when they play Buffalo, the most convenient place to stop is at the Hotel Francis, directly opposite the New York City depot."

The Billboard's editor noted that, "Eddie Green writes something besides letters. He wrote "A Good Man is Hard to Find," "Don't Let No One Man Worry Your Mind," "You Can't Keep a Good Girl Down," "Algiers," and "Blind Man's Blues." He also has written himself into a class of regular fellows with the above letter."

Eddie was an ambitious, considerate, concerned, caring, affable man, who took pride in himself and his talent. He was a meticulous dresser, and believed in being a gentleman at all times. He believed in acquiring as much knowledge about whatever he was trying to accomplish, so as not having to rely on others to secure his place in society. Though Eddie was my father, I have almost no memory of him, as he died when I was only three years old, so I cannot speak on the type of man he was, other than through the eyes of those who knew him, both personally and professionally. I don't think there is anyone left from the east coast, who knew him before 1940, where most of his career rise took place. Being born in 1891, by the time he made it to the stage, he was actually older than—or the same age as—those with whom he worked. Newspapers of the day gave Eddie kudos for his character, and he always seemed to elicit positive opinions.

Eddie was becoming a busy man. On January 12, 1921, he appeared at the Orpheum Theater in Paterson, New Jersey. By February, he had become a music publisher. On April, 1921, *The Billboard* noted that due to the success of said business, he would be moving into larger quarters on West 46th Street, New York.

During this time, Eddie wrote four more songs: "You Can Read My Letters, But You Sure Can't Read My Mind," "You've Got What I Like," "Sun Down," and "The World's All Wrong." The music for "The World's All Wrong" was written by Cuney Conner, a music writer and musical director, who was also Eddie's representative.

Eddie's newest songs caught the interest once again of Sophie Tucker, who commissioned special band arrangements for "The World's All Wrong" and "You Can Read My Letters, But You Sure Can't Read My Mind," saying the songs were a big hit in her production. She also had Eddie write a special version of "You've Got What I Like" for one of her performances.

"*Girls De Looks*" was still going strong. In February, Eddie, now performing in blackface as a character man, sang and danced at the Majestic, Jersey City, as a supporting actor, with Watson and Cohan as the main attraction. In 1921, Blacks were allowed to appear on stage with Whites if they wore blackface. Minstrel shows were popular and that was the only way for Blacks to get into mainstream show business. On April 9, 1921, Eddie appeared in *Girls De Looks*, billed as a singer of his own songs. Another *The Billboard* article from this month says the review for Eddie (Simp) Green was, ". . . very favorable and that Eddie was a good business man as well, as he has his own publishing business at 131 West 135th Street, New York."

12

Barney Gerard's first production of *Girls De Looks* in the 1921 fall season was a big attraction on the Columbia Wheel. With Watson and Cohan heading the company, "*Girls De Looks*" was to take Eddie to the Gayety in Buffalo, where he was lauded as being "one of the best dancers of men of color who had yet come to Buffalo." Eddie was to perform in *Girls De Looks* through the 1921-1922 season, garnering kudos for his performance as a soft-shoe and acrobatic dancer.

Chapter Four

An Entrepreneur in Burlesque

On October 22, 1921, the following article appeared in *The Billboard*: "Eddie Green, the erstwhile Burlesque comedian, writes from Washington to advise that he has become the president of a $200,000 motion picture company. The company, known as the Deanwood, will have a studio at Deanwood, in the District of Columbia, and promises to have pictures ready for release in the coming spring." Eddie sent out an invite, via the newspapers, for "anyone in the profession to make the offices of Deanwood their headquarters when playing Washington, D.C."

Eddie's business was listed in the *10th Annual Edition, 1922-23, First Colored Professional, Clerical, Skilled and Business Directory of Baltimore City,* which could be bought at the *Afro-American* office on Eutaw Street and Druid Hill Avenue, where Mr. R. W. Coleman, was publisher. The Deanwood Motion Pictures Corporation, was listed at 308 Southern Aid Building, Washington, D. C., with Edward Green as President. The Deanwood Motion Pictures Corporation's tagline was: Anything That You Want to Know About Moving Pictures, Write Us. [According to the Washingtonian MLK Library Division (DCPL), the address for the Southern Aid Building is now 1901 7th Street NW. The building is considered a historical landmark and is now occupied by Wells Fargo.]

I can only assume that Eddie's wife and child were in Washington, D. C.

with him in 1921, as it seems that he was indeed living there. His Deanwood Motion Pictures Corporation was short-lived. My mother did tell me that there was a time when a partner of Eddie's absconded with their money, but she had no real details. Though this may have been a set-back, as usual, Eddie never stopped moving forward. He continued writing comedy sketches and songs, while performing on the circuit in two separate plays for the next couple of years.

The Billboard March 25, 1922 gave kudos to three performers, one of them being Eddie Green of *Girls De Looks*. The person who wrote the article said, "If there were more actors in Burlesque who respected themselves as much as Eddie Green and conducted themselves as well on and off the stage there would be less criticism of Burlesque." This article says "on and off the stage." I can take from that phrase that Eddie conducted himself well at all times. They say that "character counts," and his ability to stay positive is a testament to this phrase. He was to receive many compliments in this vein over the years.

In May 1922, Eddie's tour with *Girls De Looks* ended, after which he signed up again with producer Barney Gerard for one of his Unit shows on the Shubert Circuit, writing special lyrics for the show's use and writing his own comedic sketches. October and November saw him with Town Talk Unit at the Astoria Theater, and in December, he appeared at the Dunbar Theater, having finished out his Shubert Vaudeville gig.

On February 16, 1923, a fascinating historical discovery was made. An English Archeologist, Howard Carter, found and opened King Tut's Tomb, after seven years of fruitless searching. On November 26, 1923, Howard Carter opened the second sealed door to the tomb. The next month, Eddie wrote "King Tut's Blues," with music and arrangement by Mr. Benton Overstreet, which Eddie copyrighted on June 20, 1923. The music arranger of "King Tut's Blues," Mr. Benton Overstreet, was a Vaudevillian and composer, who also wrote that well-known song, "There'll Be Some Changes Made."

Eddie's next musical writings for 1923 were "The Right Key, But the

PRODUCER CLOSES DEAL FOR ALL RACE FILMS

ddie Green, left, famous comedian who has gone for the production of movie shorts as head of e "Sepia Arts" Pictures company, closed a deal ith the Apollo theatre chain theatres for the re-ase of his flickers Saturday.. Here he is shown gning exclusive release papers with Jimmy Mar-

shall, right, manager of the Apollo theatre, while Leonard Harper looks on. Frank Schiffman, owner of the Apollo, who authorized the purchase, was high in his praise of the first release, "Dress Rehearsal," after Friday's prevue.

Eddie Green with Leonard Harper. Newspaper
headline said, "Producer closes deal for all race films."

Wrong Keyhole," and "Previous." "The Right Key, But the Wrong Keyhole" was subsequently recorded by the Okeh record label, with the song being performed by Virginia Liston, with piano accompaniment by Clarence Williams.

In April 1923, a new play titled *Plantation Days,* presented by Leonard Harper, premiered at the Lafayette Theater, with Eddie as the featured comedian for the summer run, under the direction of the Coleman Brothers. There was the "jazziest whirl of songs, dances and music ever presented."

Leonard Harper, born in 1899 in Birmingham, Alabama, began his career as a child dancer, after which he became a choreographer and producer of theater and Broadway shows. He worked with such celebrities as May West, Bill Robinson, Louis Armstrong, and Lena Horne, to name a few. Over the next ten years, Leonard and Eddie would work together on at least two additional projects. Leonard Harper died February 4, 1943.

Seemingly, Eddie never slept. In June, he found time to write and stage *Playing the Numbers,* which featured a "chorus of Creole Vamps." The play opened at the Lafayette Theatre in New York for a three-day engagement.

In the fall of 1923, Eddie began a run with Barney Gerard's *All in Fun,* at the Yorkville Theatre in New York City. The principles of this play were Will Fox and Harry Koler, as Slitkin and Slotkin. *All in Fun* was a two-act play in which the scenery went from the black and white of the interior of a jail to the setting of an Oriental harem. The plot of the play deals with two lawyers, Slitkin and Slotkin, who go from a skyscraper office in New York to a country club, and then from jail to a palace in Egypt for the wedding of Slitkin. The show included musical numbers and dancing. Eddie's performance was in blackface and with dancing, and he was also allowed to sing his own song, "Previous."

Once again, Eddie was traveling that Columbia Circuit: New York, Baltimore, Ohio, Salt Lake, Kansas City, and even San Francisco, as Barney Gerard, Eddie's boss, had procured a deal to have a West Coast Circuit. After seeing Eddie in *All in Fun,* the Sunday morning October 28, 1923 *Philadelphia Inquirer* declared him "the funniest black-skinned comic of them all."

This year was leading to a big break for Eddie, but not the biggest. He was truly on his way to becoming somebody. He was singing and dancing and providing much laughter, and he was starting to make his way into the hearts of the audience, his fellow actors, and those for whom he worked.

Chapter Five
Minsky's Little Apollo
& *A Perfect 36*

The world in 1924 just out of WWI, in the throes of the Roaring Twenties, with booze—albeit illegal booze—flowing, and folks were looking for a good time. They were ready for someone like Eddie.

A review of the Van Curler *All in Fun* show said, in part, "During the course of this show, one singing number, "Tell the Rose," Miss Kalama and Eddie Green as the dancer, was the big hit, and they were encored many times." Seems to echo back to a 1916 play that Eddie wrote.

During this time, Eddie wrote two more songs, both of which are still in copyright: "I'm Leaving You" and "I'm Sorry for It Now." Paramount recorded "I'm Sorry for it Now" with Eddie and Miss Billie Wilson. She had that old-time bluesy singing style that was perfect for this duet with Eddie. She was obviously a part of the in-crowd of 1924, as she gave a big party for Duke Ellington that year at the Crystal Caverns, a popular nightclub that catered to the city's Black population. The piano player for this tune was a Mr. Charles Matson. He was a pianist, arranger, and band-leader of the Creole Serenaders, who recorded for the Edison and Paramount labels.

Billy Minsky was, at the time, running the Little Apollo Theater, and he hired Eddie to produce stock shows every week, with his contract running through 1926. Eddie wrote and staged a new play, *Playing the Numbers*, with Henrietta Lovelace, a singer of some accord, who had appeared in Ziegfeld's *Show Boat* (1925), and, who also had a comedic act with her partner Mr. Lorenzo McLane, through the 1930s. Eddie was also working at Minsky's during the raid that inspired the musical comedy film, *The Night They Raided Minsky's* (1968), which is not exactly a claim to fame for Eddie, but the information puts Eddie's whereabouts at the time, in perspective.

The Apollo Theater building was built around 1913. It began as Hurtig and Seamon's New Burlesque Theatre with a strict "Whites only" policy. Billy Minsky took over the theater in 1928, and the theater was known as The Little Apollo. Some years later, after major closure and renovations, the theater re-opened as The Apollo Theatre in 1934, and began admitting Black patrons, and eventually introduced Showtime at the Apollo.

Eddie's work with The Apollo Theatre was impressive to those who followed such things. The *Baltimore Afro-American* dated July 4, 1925 printed this headline, "Eddie Green, East Baltimore Boy is Now Making Good." "Eddie Green Makes Stock Record, Finishes 45-Weeks Engagement with White Company in New York. Will Stage 5 Burlesque Shows. Former Member of Daly's is Now in Forefront of Profession." His success was touted as "another feather in the hat of East Baltimore."

Newspapers of this era were great champions of what they termed "race" performers. They were lucky if they were able to maintain a position on a "White" stage, obviously doing something right. That same month, Eddie was one of the comedians re-engaged by the Minsky brothers to head Minsky's Harlem stock company starting that coming August.

By September 1925, Eddie was appearing in two shows a day during the third season of Minsky's Harlem stock, in a show called *Sweet Snookies*, and it was probably best to be near the theater. During this time, Eddie moved his mother, Janie, into Harlem.

Eddie's contract with Minsky ran through 1926. March found him doubling from The Apollo, appearing at Ciro's in *The Creole Follies*. A *Variety* article found his performance less than stunning, stating, "Eddie is terribly slow in his Bert Williams delivery, but when singing he clearly articulates." [Bert Williams was a renowned Vaudeville entertainer and one of the most popular comedians of that era, a best-selling Black recording artist, and the first Black American to take a lead role on the Broadway stage.]

In 1928, Chappy Gardner wrote in his column, *Along the Rialto,* in the *Pittsburgh Courier:* "Eddie Green, well-known songwriter, electrician, motion picture operator, famed comedian, opened on the Burlesque wheel this season. Played at Newark last week in *A Perfect 36.* Eddie appeared with the regular cast, being the only race performer, but was at his best in his single that wowed the customers. Eddie for years played at The Apollo on West 125th Street where he drilled white choruses in doing race dances. He is a fine sort of modern show man."

Chapter Six

Eddie's Biggest Break

George and Connie Immerman emigrated with their brother Louie, from Germany. The Immerman's started out operating a Harlem delicatessen before opening Connie's Inn, a New York City nightclub, on Seventh Street. In 1929, George Immerman came up with the idea of Connie's *Hot Chocolates*, an all-Black revue.

Connie's *Hot Chocolates* opened at the Hudson Theater on Broadway on June 20, 1929. The show was staged by Leonard Harper, with songs by Andy Razaf and Thomas "Fats" Waller. Eddie was hired as the chief comedy writer for *Hot Chocolates*, and he also doubled as one of the performers. For *Hot Chocolates*, Andy collaborated with "Fats" Waller on "Ain't Misbehavin'," "Honeysuckle Rose," and "What Did I Do to be so Black and Blue." *Hot Chocolates* also featured Louis Armstrong, a young, up-and-coming trumpet player, in his Broadway debut, playing a trumpet solo of "Ain't Misbehavin'." Connie's *Hot Chocolates* was hailed by critics and was touted as being fast, funny and frank. *Hot Chocolates* would go on to a run of 219 performances

Andy Razaf was the son of the Grand Duke of Madagascar. He was born in Washington, D. C. as Andriamanantena Paul Razafinkarefo. The French invasion of Madagascar left his father dead, and forced his pregnant fifteen-year-old mother to escape to the United States, where he was born in 1895.

The leading male performer was dancer and comedian Jazzlips Richardson. The cast also included comedians Billy Higgins, Billy Maxey, and Baby Cox, a jazz dancer and singer, who had also performed with Duke Ellington. There was Miss Edith Wilson, who had begun her career at fifteen years of age, and had since toured the continent as a vocalist. She sang "Black and Blue." The first night cast included in the ensemble Louis Armstrong, Jimmie Baskette, Baby Cox, Eddie Green, Billy Higgins, The Jubilee Singers, and Jazzlips Richardson.

One of the skits written by Eddie was "Big Business," a comedy about a fixed prize-fight for the "in-between-weight" championship, with Eddie playing the fight manager, Billy Higgins playing the promoter, Billy Maxey as a reporter, and Jazzlips Richardson played the fighter, "Kid Licorice."

There is a recording on Victor Records of *Big Business*, a "talking song," with Eddie, Billy Higgins and Company, and "Fats" Waller on piano, with speaker parts being done by Eddie, Billy Higgins, Billy Maxey, J. E. Lightfoot, Dick Campbell, and Jazzlips Richardson. Billy Higgins had performed in the Broadway musical comedy *How Come?* (1923), and Jazzlips Richardson would have a role in Warner Bros. *The Green Pastures* (1935).

Dick Campbell began his career as a singer and straight man in Vaudeville. Beginning in 1929, he worked regularly in various stage productions in Harlem and on Broadway. Eddie and Dick would work together as comedians through 1939. Dick became a co-founder of the Negro Actors Guild, and was a producer and director for the American National Theater Association.

There was also the skit which became a popular favorite, "Sending a Wire." Written by Eddie, the skit featured him with Jimmie Baskette as a customer and clerk, respectively, in a telegraph office, where Eddie is trying to send a telegraph. The *New York Age* called "Sending a Wire" "riotously funny." Evidently, Eddie was "knocking them ga-ga" in his telegraph skit at the Hudson Theater. This skit would prove to be a big success and another stepping stone for him. Jimmie Baskette would later begin using his given name, James, and would work with Eddie again over the years. [In 1946, James Baskette was cast as Uncle Remus Walt Disney's *Song of the South.*]

"Sending a Wire" was filmed by Warner Bros. in one of their earliest Vitaphone films that featured synchronized sound. It was said to be the funniest Vitaphone comedy act "which has yet been produced," and that it "kept thousands shaking with laughter." The film is registered in the Library of Congress as *Sending a Wire*, Eddie Green and Co.

Eddie Green in *Sending a Wire* (1929). Photo courtesy of The Vitaphone Project.

"Sending a Wire" went on to be shown at Loew's Main St. New Rochelle Theater, featured after the Hearst Metrotone News, and was also screened at the Strand Theater on the same program as a Mickey Mouse cartoon called, *The Jazz Fool.* Okeh Records recorded "Sending a Wire" with Eddie Green and Company, and released it on two 78 rpm records as "'Sending a Wire' – Part 1 and Part 2, performed by Eddie Green – Monologue."

At about the same time in another part of town, *The Gannet Newspapers*, which, at the time included the *Albany News* and *The Knickerbocker Press*, decided to put together a stellar list of entertainers to perform over radio stations WGY and WHAM, to be broadcast to "Little America" for the enjoyment of Commander Richard E. Byrd, an America Naval Officer, and his explorers, who had started an expedition to the Antarctic, and had set up the "Little America" base camp on the Ross Ice Shelf. Eddie was added to the broadcast to perform his famous Telegraph skit. The broadcast also included Ralph Rainger, the composer of "Moanin' Low," Rudy Vallee, Fred Allen, and comedian Ted Healy.

Regarding Eddie's performance on the radio program, here's what *The Brooklyn Daily Eagle* said: "The whole town is talking about Eddie Green, prime colored comic, who will put on one of the funniest skits on the stage. He will dash from the Hudson Theater immediately after the final curtain to the National Broadcasting Company where he will re-enact his side-splitting "Telegraph Office" skit for Commander Byrd and his crew."

During 1929, Eddie took the time to write nine more songs in collaboration with a friend by the name of Fred Watson:

- "Her u-kee-el," a talking song, words and music by Eddie Green, with arrangement by Fred Watson.

- "Kitties (The) Band," a talking song, words and music by Eddie Green, with arrangement by Fred Watson.

- "Miller (The) o'the Glen," a talking song, words and music by Eddie Green, with arrangement by Fred Watson.

- "Red! Red! Red!," a talking song, words and music by Eddie Green, music arranged by Fred Watson.

- "She Was a Lovely Girl," a talking song, words and music by Eddie Green, arrangement by Fred Watson.

- "That Didna Trouble Me," a talking song, words and music by Eddie Green, music arranged by Fred Watson.

- "U-ie-i-o," words and music by Eddie Green, music arranged by Fred Watson.

- "We All Want What We Want, When We Want It," written and composed by Eddie Green, music arrangement by Fred Watson.

- "You Never Can Tell," a talking song, words and music by Eddie Green, arrangement by Fred Watson.

- "Elinor," words and music by Eddie Green, arrangement by Frederic Watson.

Chapter Seven

Onward and Upward

Connie's *Hot Chocolates* ran through December, 1929. On January 11, 1930, according to the *Schenectady Gazette*, there was another entertainment program sponsored by the *Buffalo Evening News* for Commander Byrd and his crew. The program featured Eddie and "Chick" Hunter, comedian and straight-man, in two sketches, *The Miser's Gold* and *Takin' a Movin' Picture*. Eddie was also given a chance to sing the song he had written in 1924, "Previous."

Warner Bros. made the decision to film Eddie in another Vitaphone film short titled *Temple Bells*, along with Ted Blackmon. *Temple Bells* was a Chinese fantasy, touted as "a highly enjoyable ten-minute Vitaphone act," with "Eddie Green, the noted colored comedian and Ted Blackmon, who played the part of a Chinaman." [*Temple Bells* is archived at the Wisconsin Historical Society.]

Somewhere along the line, Eddie and his wife Julia had split up. According to the 1930 census, Julia and their daughter, Hilda, were living in Pennsylvania, and Eddie was living in New York with Anna, his new wife. Anna was born in England, and had emigrated with her parents, who were from Russia, to the United States in 1905, when Anna was four years old. As was noted in the census, Anna was an entertainer in a nightclub, and Eddie was an actor in a show.

Eddie and Anna split up, and on January 7, 1932, Eddie, now forty-one years old, married for the third time. The new Mrs. Green, whose name was Constance, was a native of Trenton, New Jersey, and was twenty-four years old. Constance, though interested in show business, decided to become a stay-at-home wife. Eddie and Constance would remain married through the early 1940s.

During this period, Eddie was approached by producer Lee Posner with the offer to appear in and to provide help with writing the book for a play titled *Blackberries of 1932*, which had been conceived by Posner. With words and music by Thomas Peluso and Donald Heywood, and staging by Ben Bernard, Posner brought the play to the Liberty Theater for Easter. Along with Eddie as the principal comedian, there was Tim Moore, and a cast that included Mantan Moreland, Pigmeat Markham, Jackie Mabley, Monte Hawley, Baby Goins, and Sam Wooding's Orchestra.

Tim Moore was born Harry R. Moore in 1887. He ran away from home at a young age and became quite popular as a Vaudevillian and as a comedian. By 1915, Moore was performing a show he had written and staged called *The Chicago Follies* at the Booker Washington Theater in St. Louis. He was said to be "without peer." He would go on to appear in Lew Leslie's *Blackbirds* in 1929, and he headed the cast of *Black Magic* with Billy Higgins, before landing a part in *Blackberries of 1932*. Tim Moore became a household name as the bombastic "Kingfish" in the 1950s CBS television program, *Amos n Andy*. He died in 1958 at the age of seventy-one. His friends remembered him as a generous, kind man.

Jackie Mabley was later to become known as "Moms" Mabley. Jackie "Moms" Mabley was one of the top women doing stand-up at the time, eventually recording more than twenty albums of comedy routines. She appeared in movies, on television, and in nightclubs. She became known as "Moms," because she was indeed a "Mom" to many other comedians on the circuit in the 1950s and 1960s.

Mantan Moreland, born on September 3, 1902, was an actor, comedian, and movie producer. He worked in minstrel shows and Vaudeville, moving on to continuous work in movies, which included his role as the chauffer Birmingham Brown in the *Charlie Chan* movies, as well as what were then called "race" movies, *The Green Pastures* (1936), and *Cabin in the Sky* (1943). In 1946, Mantan was cast as lead in *Mantan Messes Up*, directed by Sam Newfield. The movie also starred Lena Horne, Monty Hawley, and Eddie Green. He appeared in *The Watermelon Man* in the 1970s and in a television episode of *Adam-12*, among others. Mantan Moreland passed away on September 28, 1973.

Dewey "Pigmeat" Markham, born April 18, 1904, was an entertainer. Though best known as a comedian, Markham was also a singer, dancer, and actor. His nickname came from a stage routine in which he declared himself to be "Sweet Poppa Pigmeat." In 1933, he appeared at The Apollo with Eddie. Eddie sang, and Pigmeat and Jimmie Baskette provided the jokes. In 1936, the "Pigmeat Truck" was all the rage. This truckin' dance step was Pigmeat's version of the Cotton Club's peckin' dance. Pigmeat appeared in several films, one of which he directed and starred in, *Mr. Smith Goes Ghost* (1940). In 1950 Pigmeat was one of the entertainers at the west side branch of the YMCA in Mount Vernon, New York. Along with Pigmeat was George Wiltshire, Eddie's straight man from the 1936 RCA-NBC television demonstration.

The phrase "Heah come de judge" was first used by Pigmeat on *The Ed Sullivan Show* in the 1950s and became his signature line. However, the phrase did not become popular until used by Sammy Davis, Jr. on the *Rowan and Martin's Laugh-In* television program in 1967. Pigmeat became a regular on *Laugh-In* in 1968 as the Judge. He also made appearances on *The Mike Douglas Show* and *Johnny Carson*. Dewey "Pigmeat" Markham was seventy-seven years old when he died in 1981.

Montrose Westin Hawley, also known as Monte Hawley, was born on October 25, 1901. He was a stage and top screen actor of his time. He was cast in the Broadway play, *Shuffle Along* (1921), a musical that ran for 504 performances, and in a number of independent Black-cast films, such as *The Duke is Tops* (1938) and *Mantan Messes Up* (1946). Monte Hawley died in New York City in 1950.

Blackberries of 1932 was something less than a hit, as there were only seven showings. I believe this was the first time Eddie worked with Mantan Moreland, but it would not be the last. Eddie would also appear in *Mantan Messes Up* (1946) with Monte Hawley.

During March 1932, a kidnapping occurred that proved catastrophic for our nation. Charles Lindbergh's twenty-month-old son was kidnapped from his nursery in New Jersey. There were a number of songs written during this time about the kidnapping, one of which was titled "Find That Darling Baby." Eddie wrote the music in collaboration with Morton Levine, and the words were written by Frank Ceinta and W. A. Wright. The Lindbergh kidnapping ended tragically, when the body of the little baby was found on May 12, 1932.

Later that year, "Eddie Green, of musical comedy fame" was in rehearsal for a musical revue, *Brighton Follies of 1932,* once again working with Will Cohan and Joseph K. Watson, with whom he worked in *All in Fun* (1924). The rehearsals were being held at New Brighton Theater in Florida. Fame had reached Eddie.

On September 5, 1933, *Temptations of 1933* opened the season for Minsky's Brooklyn Theater, featuring Eddie Green. The audience got a new treat, with two shows between 10:00 a.m. and 5:00 p.m. And on September 18, 1933, the Brooklyn Theater celebrated its first anniversary by featuring sixty-five players, Eddie included, in a two-act Burlesque extravaganza titled *Red Hot Tots.*

After the close of *Red Hot Tots,* Eddie found various opportunities to showcase his brand of humor. The next year on April 6, 1934, The General Tire Revue debuted its first show of their series. Jack Benny was the host for this season, with Don Wilson, Frank Parker, and Mary Livingstone. On August 3, 1934, Eddie was cast as the train porter, while Jack and the gang solved The Stooge Murder Case during a train ride.

During this same time period, there was a popular radio program titled, *The Raymond Knight Cuckoo Hour,* also known as *The KUKU Hour,* which showcased Raymond Knight's satirical type of humor. In June, *The Herald Statesman* announced, "Eddie Green and Dick Campbell, Negro comedians," as guests of *The KUKU Hour.*

Raymond Knight was an actor, comedian, and comedy writer, who was hired by the NBC Blue Network specifically because of his brand of humor. *The KUKU Hour* aired from approximately 1929 through 1936.

By October, Eddie was back working at The Apollo, when it was announced that he would be held over due to his popularity and versatility. Eddie was cast by producer and choreographer Clarence Robinson in a production of his show, *Christmas Carols,* on December 22, 1934, at The Apollo. Heading the stage bill along with Eddie were Jackie Mabley, Pigmeat Markham, Jimmie Baskette, and The Sixteen Apollo Rockettes, with Ralph Cooper as emcee.

Chapter Eight

In His Element

Eddie, now living on 138th Street, in New York, landed a spot on a WEAF NBC national hook-up, starring Charles Winninger as Captain Henry. *The Pittsburgh Courier* noted on June 22, 1935, "Eddie Green, billed on Broadway and elsewhere as ace among sepia Black-face comedians, has been signed for twenty-six weeks to co-feature on a bill with Ernest Whitman and Charles Winninger, which will be aired every Sunday night from 10:00 to 11 o'clock over WEAF. Radio comedy is by far nothing new to Eddie Green who, for several seasons worked very successfully with Rudy Vallee, in fact so successfully until he was returned three times by popular demand. Leaving the Vallee hour more than a year ago, he worked through a long term contract engagement at the Apollo Theater, where with his original style of getting laughs he won an uncountable following among Harlem's theater-going masses."

The radio comedy program was the Maxwell House *Show Boat* radio program, inspired by the Jerome Kern-Oscar Hammerstein II's musical, *Show Boat,* which opened on Broadway in 1927. Charles Winninger had played the role of Cap'n Andy Hawks in the stage performance, which was the inspiration to play the role of "Captain Henry" on the NBC Maxwell House program. Maxwell House *Show Boat* was the top radio show in the United States from 1933 to about 1937.

Charles J. Winninger, born May 26, 1884, was a stage and film actor, most often cast in comedies or musicals, but equally at home in drama. Charles Winninger also starred in *Uncle Charlie's Tent Show* with Eddie and Ernest Whitman. The show's tag line was "New Hour Brings to Listeners the Modern Tent Show with old-time glamour," and their cast consisted of Charles Winninger as Uncle Charlie, Eddie Green as Jerry, and Ernest Whitman as Sam.

Ernest Whitman, born in Fort Smith, Arkansas on February 21, 1893, was a stage and screen actor, who appeared in *Green Pastures, Cabin in the Sky*, and *The Lost Weekend*, just to name a few movies. Mr. Whitman died in Hollywood, California August 5, 1954.

Eddie also got the chance to share the stage with the Nicholas Brothers, and Willie Bryant in a Leonard Harper musical comedy. A newspaper article from October 19, 1935, stated that Eddie was "notoriously funny."

Eddie was appearing periodically, along with comedienne Helen Lynd and Frank Fay on Rudy Vallee's radio show, *The Fleischmann's Yeast Hour*, over radio station WEAF-NBC, performing skits written by John Tucker Battle, which had made him a favorite to the fans. The skits were a part of the "Heroes Wuz People" section of the radio program, and were done in what the newspapers called, "Negro dialect." John Tucker Battle, would become well-known in Hollywood as a screenwriter, working on *The Fleischmann's Yeast Hour* and such shows as *Bat Masterson* and *Have Gun, Will Travel*.

The Fleischmann's Yeast Hour was a pioneering musical variety radio program broadcast on NBC from 1929 to 1936, when it became *The Royal Gelatin Hour*, continuing until 1939. The program was sponsored by Fleischmann's Yeast, a popular brand of yeast.

April 16, 1936, the *Albany Evening News*, printed an article with the headline, "Eddie Green Brings Fun to Air Tonight," referring to Eddie as "That sad-voiced Negro comedian," the article said that Eddie's performance of the John Tucker Battle's *Legend of Miles and Priscilla Standish* that past week was "distinctly good fun and a bit out of the ordinary for radio."

Joe Bostic, of *The New York Age*, in his April 18, 1936 Radiograph column, sub-titled "Peak Radio Performance of the Week," noted, ". . . the choice of Eddie Green's performance as the best of the week is the second time within a month he has been accorded this honor." Mr. Bostic was referring to the past Thursday night's "Vallee Show." He further stated, "Eddie Green, it seems to be is more than a new star in the radio firmament, he's a symbol of what race artists might achieve if they have a distinctive and individual entertainment idea to offer." Mr. Bostic finishes his article with, "We doff our hat to a sterling performer and a great fellow."

Mr. Bostic saw Eddie as a "great fellow," which, to me, seems a part of that which helped Eddie progress in this business. It was, perhaps, not about overcoming racism or overlooking other's issues with Eddie as a Black man, but instead was about talent, knowledge, and character. It was also about hard work. Eddie was a man who put his whole self into every aspiration.

To digress for a bit, on March 27, 1936 *The Kingston Daily Freeman, New York,* printed an article in which there was posted a picture of the late Hiram Percy Maxim, noted scientist and inventor, founder and first President of the American Radio Relay League, and the International Amateur Radio Union in Hartford, Connecticut. The article, written by Clinton B. DeSoto, discussed the ability of everyday people to help one another through the use of Amateur Radio. He wrote of some 40,000 of these folks being in the United States. That these people, from age eight to eighty, had been granted licenses by the Federal Communications Commission (FCC), following rigid examination covering radio theory, technique, and laws. He writes of the part Mr. and Mrs. General Public had in the World War, that Uncle Sam was able to use the competent observers by them staying in constant touch with expeditions at the remote corners of the earth when no other means availed, including parties such as Admiral Byrd, Commander Macmillan, and Captain Bartlett.

He mentioned the wealthy Henry B. Joy, retired Detroit capitalist and financier and past President of the Packard Motor Co. Mr. DeSoto stated that "there is hardly any occupational category that is not represented, filling station attendants, bellhops, miners," and he also mentioned a few celebrities, Freeman Gosden (Amos of *Amos 'n' Andy*), and "Eddie Green, well-known Harlem radio artist and entertainer."

Here was an article that pointed out to me the fact that Eddie was well-known at the time, whereas, today, he is virtually non-existent, lost from memory, with his achievements lost with him. As a man who came from literally nothing to rise to the heights he achieved, I think Eddie deserves to be brought back to the forefront of the minds of today's readers, especially as this book provides a "new" look at a past celebrity.

Eddie's passion, as far as hobbies go, was amateur ham radio. He was a government-licensed amateur, with the radio call letters W2AKM, which he had engraved on a pin for the lapel of his suits. Eddie had a set up in his Buick for long trips and a radio station in the basement of our home in the late1940s. Eddie would also perform at conventions of the amateur radio club in Long Island, New York.

Chapter Nine

RCA/NBC

E ddie said that his biggest break came in 1929. I think his next big break, and a first for the history books, occurred on July 7, 1936, when RCA and NBC presented their first demonstration television broadcast.

In preparing for its first field-test television transmission, NBC converted a radio studio in the RCA Building (now the GE Building) in New York City Rockefeller Center for television. The transmitter was installed in one of the upper floors of the Empire State Building with the antenna on the mooring mast, 1,285 feet above street level. Two links interconnected the studio and transmitter. One of these was an underground coaxial cable approximately a mile in length; the other was a radio link.

At the request of Mr. David Sarnoff, the head of RCA and NBC, one of the largest corporations in the world, RCA provided a test of their electronic technology with their first attempt at actually programming a 30-minute variety show featuring speeches, dance ensembles, monologues, vocal numbers, and film clips. The program was specially broadcast to a select group of listeners and watchers.

On June 29, 1936, NBC began field-test television transmissions from W2XF/W2XJ to an audience of some 75 receivers in the homes of high-level RCA staff and a dozen or so sets in a closed circuit viewing room in the 52nd floor offices of the RCA Building.

The first public demonstration of these field trials took place on July 7, 1936 to RCA's 225 licensees. Major General J. G. Harbord, Chairman of the Board of RCA, announced that there were three sets in operation at the time, the most distant in Harrison, New Jersey.

An article in the *Pittsburgh Courier* announced the appearance of "Eddie Green, and his partner George Wiltshire, on the television demonstration. Eddie Green, popular stage, radio, and screen comedian, and George Wiltshire, well-known 'straight man,' were the two men of color chosen to lend their bit to the first television broadcast by the Radio Corporation of America from their studios last Tuesday."

The first part of this two-part program begins with General James G. Harbord, who had resigned as President of RCA and was, in 1936, Chairman of the Board of RCA, and David Sarnoff seated at a desk discussing their "baby"—television. The second part begins with Milton J. Cross making the following announcement: "Good afternoon, ladies and gentlemen, I am very delighted to be allowed to participate in this demonstration on television. For your dedication, we draw on that droll comic, Eddie Green and his partner, George Wiltshire, offering a little philosophical erudition."

Out walks my father in blackface—my first look at Eddie alive in blackface. I was shocked. My mother had told me that Eddie had never appeared in blackface because he believed blackface was demeaning. Yet, there he was. I don't know if this was an assumption on my mother's part, or if Eddie actually told her this. Of course, sixty years later, it really no longer matters. The sketch consisted of Eddie telling George funny stories about his cold weather antics, his mother-in-law, and his grandfather. Mom had passed on by the time I discovered a copy of this film on-line.

I was inspired, however, to do some research on the blackface comedian, and I came away with a much better understanding of why Eddie chose to use this medium as a way to further his career, as opposed to possibly never getting the chance to achieve his goals. I admire my father for having the courage to pursue that which he found important in his life.

Part two of this film also included some dancing girls and Ed Wynn, a very funny Vaudeville comedian. Mr. Wynn, at the beginning of his act, said that he was honored to be asked to appear on the very first television broadcast in the world. Of course, we know now that Ed Wynn went on to great heights in the entertainment business, but how many people are aware that he was the voice of "Fred the Lion" in *Super Chicken*, a cartoon show I definitely remember from my childhood. Mr. Wynn also appeared in *The Diary of Ann Frank* (1959), *Mary Poppins* (1964) as Uncle Albert, *The Absent Minded-Professor* (1961) as the Fire Chief, and dozens of other films and television series.

George Wiltshire, Eddie's straight man, born in 1900, was an actor and comedian, who first appeared on Broadway in the *Hot Rhythm* revue at the Times Square Theater. Before appearing on the RCA test broadcast, he had also worked with The Apollo "Amateur Hour" in 1935. George Wiltshire was not only one of the great "straight men" in show business, he also appeared in movie productions, including *Keep Punching* (1939) opposite Canada Lee, *It Happened in Harlem* (1945), *Midnight Menace* (1946), and *Junction 88* (1947). He would go on to appear in many television shows, specifically, *Sanford and Son* (1976) starring Red Foxx, in which he appeared as Elroy Pitt, a sidekick of Mr. Foxx's character, "Fred" Sanford. It was said that one of George's first dreams of the acme of success was to work at John T. Gibson's Standard Theater, which is where Eddie started back in 1900. George's talent carried him much further. He died in Los Angeles in 1976.

The RCA/NBC television test was only given a small space in the local newspapers, maybe because television was not seen, as yet, to be a big deal by a lot of people. But those who knew the potentialities of television made sure the right people were televised.

Within the next few months, Eddie was asked to perform his specific brand of comedy on various radio programs, such as, *The Art of Conversation*, *Dr. Jekyll and Mr. Hyde*, and *Captain Kidd*. During the month of September, he made two appearances on Rudy Vallee's radio show, one airing from the

Canadian National Convention, where Vallee and his Connecticut Yankees were playing a two-week engagement. Boris Karloff did a dramatic sketch, and Eddie did another John Tucker Battle sketch titled "Adam and Eve."

Eddie's next appearance on September 9, 1936, featured Eddie as Captain Kidd, in another John Tucker Battle sketch. Another *Heroes Wuz People* skit, "Romeo and Juliette," didn't go over so well, prompting the *Albany Evening News* to give it a "fair to middling" review.

Eddie's appearance on an Edison Company program elicited a completely different response. Joe Bostic, writer of the column "Radiograph," had this to say about Eddie: "Eddie Green, Harlem's funster, who was guest star at the premier of the *Echoes of New York Town* program, presented by the Consolidated Edison Company appeared again on the program, Eddie proved beyond a doubt that he is the ace Negro comic of the air."

Most people, so far, enjoyed Eddie's droll humor when presenting his *Heroes Wuz People* sketches. One such person was Franklyn Frank of the *Associated Negro Press*. Frank's column was titled "All Quiet on the Protestin' Front." He began one of his columns with a discussion of why there had been no debates, lately, on how folks felt about the *Amos 'n' Andy* radio show, how quiet everyone had become. By everyone, he was addressing the "race" folks and how they were saying little about radio activity. He said, too, that the praisers, as opposed to the protestors, could "hold a convention in a telephone booth."

Mr. Frank then begins to discuss Eddie, "This brings up the subject of Eddie Green, the fine comedian who appears occasionally on the *Rudy Vallee* hour. Eddie, who specializes in burlesques of famous plays and men of history, is one of the few people of color ever to win such radio recognition as a comic. Thus far, even the most thin-skinned of Duskymericans can find no reasonable grounds for objection to his style." Mr. Franks was concerned that no one was writing in to the radio programs, praising someone like Eddie, who managed to achieve a good deal of recognition through his comedic style and talent, as opposed to writing in and protesting those Black people who worked on *Amos 'n' Andy*, allowing themselves to be caricatured or stereotyped.

That Eddie elicited this type of recognition, gives me an insight into how Eddie projected himself during his performances. In later years, one of Eddie's employees would state that Eddie was the same person, on and off the screen, so it was probably true of Eddie on and off the radio. He was confident and comfortable with himself.

Chapter Ten

His Expanding World

In January 1937, Eddie was added to *The Royal Gelatin Hour* permanently. This year, when Mr. Vallee went on summer vacation, he did something different in regard to who would take over his summer spot. He insisted that Louis Armstrong host the show during his absence. This made Mr. Armstrong the first Black American to host a national network program. The *Ballston Spa Daily Journal*, Ballston Spa, New York reported, "A new variety show, an all-Negro revue, makes its debut on WJZ-NBC." Based on the hot rhythm of Harlem, as dispensed by Louis Armstrong's orchestra, together with his trumpet, the cast will include Eddie Green as the comedian, aided or abetted by Gee Gee James." Here was a gigantic boost to Eddie's career. Though Eddie was not new to radio work, being a part of a broadcast with the first Black American host, must have added new interest in him from other programs or sponsors.

Gee Gee James was an actress and comedian, who had made stage appearances on the same bill as Bessie Smith and George Wiltshire in 1933. In 1939, Gee Gee refused an invitation to the Club Plantation in St. Louis because they wanted her to enter through the kitchen door. She was sometimes described as "the female Rochester" due to her gravelly voice.

Lest we believe that everyone had cottoned to Eddie right away, I would like to mention a little blurb written by Miss Mary O'Neil, of *The Knicker-*

bocker News. Though Eddie was becoming wildly popular, this lady seemed to have other ideas, writing, on August 21, 1937, "What that Eddie Green is doing in radio, I don't know. I still can't see his type of comedy. But as I said before Vallee can't have a success every single time." Miss O'Neil was entitled to her opinion, of course, I am just glad Eddie's success did not suffer due to bad publicity. Even though, they do say that any publicity is good publicity.

There was also Mr. Aaron Stein, who wasn't particularly interested in Eddie's type of humor, until one night in 1937. In a review printed in *Radio Today*, April 19, 1937, Mr. Stein wrote, "It is with considerable misgivings that we tuned in Friday night for the new Eddie Green-Louis Armstrong sponsored series. In Mr. Armstrong's unparalleled blowing of blue notes, we had utter confidence, but Mr. Green had in his time as a guest performer on the Vallee show provided bits that led us to expect little but pain." As you might imagine, I considered leaving this out of book, but I must remain true to the reality of life. Fortunately, Mr. Stein was pleased with what he heard, he went on to write, "Against all expectations, however, Mr. Green was very funny. He did not rely on his dialect or on tricks of voice or intonation for his comic results."

The article goes on to remind the readers that, even though Eddie was best known as a stage and screen actor, he was best remembered as the radio comedian, who appeared for a number of weeks as the featured attraction of the full hour Sunday evening, NBC *Echoes of New York Town* program," and that he had "won a marked degree of success for his efforts in this spot." The writer also stated, "His portrayal of the characters selected for him to play, won the hearty approval of metropolitan radio critics among whom were such recognized authorities as Ben Gross (radio critic *"New York Daily News)* and Nick Kenny, columnist and radio critic."

Mr. Bob Hayes of *The Chicago Defender*, in his column "Here and There," began his May 22, 1937 column, thus: "It was like turning back the pages of yesteryear when we were greeted by our life-long pal, Eddie Green, NBC artist now being featured with Louis Armstrong and his Hot Harlem Review." It truly warmed my heart to read those few lines written by Mr. Hayes. Somehow, other people's memories have a way of allowing me to "see" my father, in a more personal way.

This radio gig lasted through the summer and it must have brought Eddie a nice sum of money, because by July, he had gone into the restaurant business, and on August 7, 1937, he opened the doors to his first restaurant, Eddie's "Bar-Bee-Q" eatery, located in Harlem. The restaurant was "swanky and cozy," and became a favorite rendezvous place of many celebrities.

Entrepreneurship never kept Eddie from doing what he liked best, which, I believe, was performing for a radio audience, and, therefore, Eddie joined the *Shell Chateau with Joe Cook* radio program in 1937. Joe Cook, who was born Joe Lopez, started out as a circus performer, becoming a major circus attraction. Later, Joe became a Broadway musical star, and eventually went on to become a radio personality. I believe Eddie's stint on Joe's program was short-lived, perhaps lasting one or two seasons.

Eddie's move away from Vaudeville and Burlesque and into musical comedy and then radio had been seamless. He was a music producer and had become a restaurateur. Hollywood may have sounded like the "next best place to be" for an up and coming comedian and business man, who was now forty-six years old.

Eddie, who was seen by some as a protégée of Rudy Vallee, on whose show he performed his popular "Heroes Wuz People" skits, left Harlem with his wife in August 1937 to join the *Show Boat* cast in Hollywood. *Show Boat* was a popular NBC radio program that aired on Thursday nights at 9:00 p.m. on station WEAF. Inspired by the Jerome Kern, Oscar Hammerstein II Broadway musical, the show starred Charles Winninger as Cap'n Henry, the proprietor of a river-going boat, which featured an entertainment troupe. Every Thursday night, *Show Boat* would lower the gangplank and take aboard various stars of stage and screen.

While Eddie was becoming acquainted with the west coast, a Reverend Glynn T. Settle, pastor of Gethsemane Baptist Church in Cleveland, made a decision to put together the Wings Over Jordan Choir (WOJC), the first full-time professional Black choir in America. Rev. Dr. Glenn Thomas Settle, was born October 10, 1894, in Reidsville, North Carolina, moved to Cleveland about 1920, and became a pastor in 1935.

In 1937, Rev. Settle and his choir inaugurated a successful weekly program, titled *The Negro Hour* on CBS Radio in Cleveland, reaching 40 million listeners. Proficient and versatile, during 1938 to 1949, the choir also travelled, performing before sold-out, non-segregated audiences in over forty American states, five European countries, Canada, and Mexico. On January 9, 1938, the Wings Over Jordan Choir *Negro Hour* had its national debut over the CBS network.

While Eddie was in Los Angeles, he decided to write a long letter to the editorial section of the *California Eagle,* regarding the *Negro Hour* radio program. The paper printed the letter on February 24, 1938. The following letter provides some idea of the goings on in Eddie's head in regard to his race and in regard to how he thought a radio program should be run, and shows also that he did not have a problem expressing himself:

"I am writing a letter concerning the much discussed Negro Hour. This letter may be too long for publication, but I hope not, because it is written by one who knows the radio business, so here 'tis.

"To intelligently discus any subject one should know something about that subject, so first may I introduce myself! I am known in big time radio from coast to coast, having appeared many times on the major chains and television programs. From the mechanical side, I am a government licensed Radio Operator, and I am still studying the technical side. Now to the subject under discussion. The Negro Hour. In its present state and I am judging by the program I heard this past Thursday. It was terrible. Now of course you may not like that word, but that is the only word that will describe it shortly. Now, mind you I did not say the people, I said the program. Remember the M.G.M. Maxwell House program opened with the greatest stars in the world but it was sad. What was the answer? Poor construction. In our case we have an example of poor construction, plus poor judgment. So now with our heads together let's try a little constructive criticism. First the theme song. Do you actually believe that the hour that is to represent the true negro should start with a tune that, at once brings to mind the back room of a tea pad, if you know what I mean, of course you don't. So why not take those splendid voices and find a brilliant work of some of our great Negro composers. There are many. Or you might even pick a suitable stanza from the pen of our poets (Dunbar and others), set it to music. Brilliant forceful music, and thus have a theme song that tells the world, "Here comes an upright, fearless, man" and not a low shuffling creature born of the rhythm of the gutter.

Now don't think that I mean that the program should go highbrow. It should not. But, it should stay above a certain level. In other words, a blues singer should be introduced as an artist. If only for the simple reason that she (or he) is.

"Now to the announcers; first they talk too loud. To start the show off, it is permissible, after that, NO. They must remember that they are gentlemen addressing ladies and gentlemen and if for no other reason than that, a gentleman never raises his voice. Next, they talk too fast. It's tough on the listener, and worst of all, it does not give the sponsor a real break. And don't forget that it is the sponsor who keeps the program on the air (or is it?) Why not sit down with the list of sponsors and a stop watch and read the whole thing slowly, or at least distinctly, and time it. Then time the rest of the program accordingly.

While we are at it, we might as well be professional. Build up every artist. Last week everyone in the first part of the program was built DOWN. And put back the applause. This show needs it.

"And now, sketches. By all means have them. BUT, don't take old things that have been used on other stations. One reason for this is that maybe the thing was copyrighted and you, your sponsors and the station finds themselves in what can be serious trouble. Why not do this: ask or advertise for scripts written by amateur writers. Not jokes, but little four or five minute scripts about Negro home life. You can give small prizes. At the same time, you would be encouraging our youngsters and giving them an opportunity to hear the enactment of their work. I hope you can see the great possibilities of this.

The news items were GREAT, but they should be read that way. They were the record of achievement of the Negro. They were something to be proud of. The scandal items were silly. This sort of thing never means anything unless you can call names, and that you don't dare do. And even if you could, do you really think that this is uplifting. Those few minutes could have well been given to the sponsors or more news items.

"So may I say that you have a great idea, a fine bunch of people and a healthy bunch of sponsors. Now buckle down and put some real perspiration behind the program, because in your hands fate has placed the greatest instrument for the spreading of propaganda that the world has ever known. Why not use it to advantage? And now in closing, USE THE NEGRO NEWSPAPERS to tell the people that you have a program.

"I hope that this criticism has been constructive and that it is accepted in good faith. If so, then good luck to you."

Soon after Eddie's letter was printed in *The California Eagle*, it received the following response from Charles L. Upton, which was also printed in *The California Eagle*: "Out of all the letters I have read in 'The Eagle's Feathers', the one which was published in last week's issue under the name of Eddie Green, is the only one that seems to ring true and sincere. Mr. Green, first outlines his authority and qualifications on radio programs and then points out the ways and means to correct the things that are lacking in the *Negro Hour Program*."

Eddie was a self-educated, self-made, and opinionated man, who believed in using his knowledge to help those of his own race stand tall, and to present themselves in the best possible light, in order to acquire the prominence that was their due.

Eddie returned from the coast during that summer and continued appearing with *The Royal Desserts Hour*. The *New York Post* reported on July 1, 1938, a review of that night's *Royal Desserts Hour*. "We are generally rather critical of this show, but there wasn't any possible complaint to make. We'd like to hear Eddie Green in lots more 'Heroes Wuz People' stories played as Robin Hood was last night." This program was also listed as *The Royal Desserts Hour*.

Life was beginning to get even more interesting, and Eddie would garner a lot more praise, even though the next vehicle in which he starred was considered a huge flop by critics. The play, *A Woman's A Fool to Be Clever*, concerns a woman who sees her husband being taken away from her and decides to play dumb as her way of getting him back. The acting in this play fell flat as far as the reviewers were concerned, except for Eddie. One reviewer noted that Eddie's character was invariably funny, possibly because Eddie could not "open his mouth without being amusing." Another noted that Eddie's humorous performance as the Negro servant was the one pleasant feature of the evening. Newspaper columnist Walter Winchell entrusted "a few sallies" to Eddie as the most popular member of the troupe. A mention from Walter Winchell meant a great deal in those days.

A Woman's A Fool to Be Clever opened on Broadway, at the National Theater on October 18, 1938 and closed October 22, 1938 with only seven performances. It was written by Dorothy Bennett and Link Hannah. Besides Eddie, the cast included Edwin Phillips, Ian Keith, Vera Allen, and Donald Foster.

In case there is any question, I am certainly not trying to criticize the play, only to point out the many kudos Eddie received in his travels on this entertainment path. Even my mom once mentioned the Walter Winchell comment on Eddie's performance, which tells me how impressed she was, and there was not much that impressed my mother.

To put a point on this chapter, at the beginning of December, Eddie was given a screen test for the role of "Pork" in the 20th Century Fox production of Margaret Mitchell's *Gone With The Wind*. Several other stars were also tested, including Louise Beavers and the White House cook at the time. While in Los Angeles, Eddie had the chance to meet Miss Hattie McDaniel, with whom he would later work on the *Jubilee* radio programs.

For those who may not know, Miss McDaniel is best known for her role in *Gone With The Wind* (1939) as "Mammy," for which she won the Academy Award for Best Supporting Actress, making her the first African-American woman to win an Academy Award.

Chapter Eleven
KoKo in the *Hot Mikado* at the World's Fair

The *Hot Mikado* (1939) was a musical theater adaptation of Gilbert and Sullivan's *The Mikado*, with a Black cast, produced by Mike Todd. The first production was at the Broadhurst Theater and ran from March 23, 1939 until June 3, 1939, for 85 performances. The cast included Bill "Bojangles" Robinson as the Mikado, Frances Brock as Pitti-Sing, Rosa Brown as Katisha, Maurice Ellis as Pooh-Bah, Eddie Green as KoKo, and Rosetta LeNoire as Peep-Bo. The musical was also produced at the 1939-1940 New York World's Fair.

Seeing the film of my father dancing on stage as the Lord High Executioner with Mr. Bill "Bojangles" Robinson was a blast and made me wonder why mom didn't mention this to me. According to the *Brooklyn Eagle*, when Eddie walked onto the stage the "spirit of Negro comedy comes with him."

During the month of May, time out was taken to celebrate Bill "Bojangles" Robinson's sixty-first birthday. Mike Todd gave an after-theater party that was held on stage at the Broadhurst. Eddie, on behalf of the cast, presented Mr. Robinson with a silver plaque, which read, "Happy Birthday Bill Robinson from the cast of the *Hot Mikado* Co., Broadhurst Theater, May 28, 1939."

On April 30, 1939, the World's Fair held its Grand Opening. In two seasons, 44 million people attended the exhibits. This was the first exposition to be based on the future. The opening slogan was "Dawn of a New Day." David Sarnoff, who was then President of RCA, placed a TV set on display at the opening of the World's Fair for the world to see. Eddie was mesmerized. He spent every day that he could at the World's Fair, checking out the "future." The Transportation Exhibit, electric typewriters at the IBM pavilion, Art, the AT&T Pavilion where they housed the Voder, a mechanized, synthetic voice that spoke to attendees. The President of the United States, Franklin D. Roosevelt, gave a speech that was broadcast over the radio, and the President's speech was also televised.

The *Hot Mikado*, after playing at the Hudson Theater, played at the World's Fair. Eddie usually arrived at the stage door on the run with just enough time to "whisk into those silly black-and-white puttees for his stint as Ko-ko." When he was not performing, Eddie hung around the Communication exhibits at the Fair.

My father was a well-read, intelligent man, who was involved in life in general. He made it his business to stay abreast of current events and to learn everything he could about that which would be of use in reaching his goals. I read somewhere that in order to succeed in Burlesque, actors needed to be familiar with works such as plays written by Shakespeare, because this was where they found their inspiration for, say, satirical comedy. Eddie was in that bracket.

One reviewer, to my mind, seemed to have no understanding of the preparation taken to be successful in an acting capacity, as is evidenced in this review in the *Brooklyn Eagle*: "Eddie Green, the comedian, hasn't lost any of his Negroid drollery by taking up the technicalities of the radio, operating a private station at the Hudson. Since last June, he has bought one of the finest private libraries in Harlem. If anything, he is funnier." Of course, it could be that I am just thin-skinned because this person is discussing my father. The article goes on to say, "Anyway, he gets a hilarious twist into Ko-ko that Messrs. G. and S. never thought of, and when he swings 'Titwillow' usually comes close to stopping the show. Outside of theater and radio work, owns and operates two barbeque emporiums. Serves nothing but spare ribs. Says Paul Whiteman is his best customer at the one on 7th Avenue."

In late 1939, Eddie and his homemaker wife, to whom he was "happily married," were living in New York on 138th Street. His first daughter had begun to follow in his footsteps, and, Eddie was the proud owner of the first television set in Harlem.

Chapter Twelve
Movie Mogul,
Sepia Art Pictures Company

E ddie had been busy also in another arena in which he had interests, motion pictures. He had tried in 1922 with Deanwood Motion Pictures to
realize his idea of producing motion pictures, however, this venture failed.
By early August 1939, he set up his new production company, Sepia Art Pictures Company. Sepia started out with a capital of $25,000, in New York, with
"familiar theatrical figure Eddie Green as guiding light." In my search for information, I found a letterhead from Sepia Art Pictures Company with the
motto: "Producing the Best in Moving Pictures, Of, By, and With Negroes."

The film studio was set up in Palisades, New Jersey, which later became
Fort Lee, New Jersey. Fort Lee, which was a borough at the eastern border
of Bergen County, was New Jersey's busiest production center in the early
1900s. Fort Lee was the "movie capital" before there was Hollywood.

The first permanent film studio built there was the Champion Film
Company, then Fox, followed by other studios such as Universal, Goldwyn,
and Biograph Studios, and Seiden Sound Films, owned by Joseph Seiden,
known as the Goldwyn of Flatbush. There was a diverse group of filmmakers at Fort Lee, including female filmmakers such as Alice Guy-Blaché, who
co-founded Solax Co. Many films were made at Fort Lee through the 1930s.

Today, those film studios are parking lots. Because of highly flammable nitrate film, some of the studios went up in flames. Due to war efforts, many of the early movies that were filmed at Fort Lee were recycled in an effort to recover the silver from the film. It is difficult to document anything from those Fort Lee movie-making days. However, the Fort Lee Historical Society and Fort Lee Commission are trying their best to keep those old memories alive, if nowhere else but in New Jersey.

Oscar Micheaux, author, director, and producer, earned recognition while working at Metropolitan Studios, his base of operations in the borough. In 2008, Fort Lee High School celebrated Black History Month by showcasing the history of Black filmmakers, particularly Oscar Micheaux, and the borough's extensive role in independent film.

The Sepia Art staff consisted of Ismay Yearwood, his secretary, Jack Caldwell, who was sales manager and assistant (Jack knew all the ins and outs of the movie industry, and as such made all the contacts and kept in tune with the public's tastes in film), and, Calvin Smith, a young photographer, who was studying photography at the New York Institute. There was also Miss Mamie Fleming, secretary, and Mr. Dewey Wineglass, who served as the Sepia Art Pictures talent scout. Mr. Wineglass, also known as Thompson Dewey Wineglass, was an actor, and musical comedy songwriter, who once appeared with Billy McLaurin, the gentleman who collaborated with Eddie on the song, "Blind Man's Blues."

Eddie sent his new starlets to The Dick Campbell group, where they were taught the prerequisites of acting. Mr. Campbell, as well as singing, dancing, and acting, had by now opened his own talent agency, co-founded the Negro People's Theater, with Rose McClendon, and had co-founded the Rose McClendon Players, along with his wife, Muriel Rahn, who would also walk through the doors of Sepia Art Pictures.

Eddie's cast members varied over the three-year period that he had his studio at Fort Lee, which included veteran actors, as well as those wanting to become actors. Among those who appeared in Eddie's movies were:

Amanda Randolph: Born September 2, 1896, she was an actress, singer, and musician. Miss Randolph appeared in Oscar Micheaux movies and on the radio program, *Young Dr. Malone*. She would go on to appear on the *Amos 'n' Andy* television program as "Saphhire." Miss Randolph also appeared on television as the title character in *Beulah* (1953) with Ernest Whitman. She was the first Black American performer to star in a regularly scheduled network television show.

Babe Matthews: She was a "very terrific vocalist," who sang with the Jimmie Lunceford Band, and had one song, "Why Am I So Blue," written by Joe Thomas, that listed on the charts right next to Billy Eckstine's "Prisoner of Love." As an actress, Miss Matthews also appeared in *King for a Day* (1934), and *Paradise in Harlem* (1939) with blues stylist Mamie Smith.

Bonnie Marie Skeete: She was a local Beauty contest winner.

Carol Pertlow: She was discovered by Dewey Wineglass in Newark, New Jersey. She was working in a newspaper office writing columns on North Jersey socialites. Mr. Wineglass recognized her as being the past winner of a statewide newspaper contest and knew that she had been crowned "Miss Sepia New Jersey" at the Rockland Palace in New York. Mr. Wineglass suggested Carol take a screen test, because she was "the perfect type of the innocent young girl."

Dick Campbell: Of the Dick Campbell Talent Agency, he was also a singer, dancer, and an actor.

Elinor Seagures: She appeared in Eddie's movie, *Comes Midnight* (1940).

'Honey Boy' Johnson: He was an actor, credited with *At the Mike*, a dancer and a comedian.

James (Jimmie) Baskette: Since working with Eddie in 1929, he had appeared in four previous movies before joining the Sepia Art Pictures cast of stars, and eventually become quite well-known through his portrayal of Uncle Remus in Walt Disney's *Song of the South* (1946).

J. Louis Johnson: He was an actor, born on March 20, 1878 in New Albany, Indiana, who would become known for the movie *Homecoming* (1948) with Clark Gable, and *Reet, Petite and Gone* (1947). He had bit parts in many movies, including Alfred Hitchcock's *Strangers on a Train* (1951). He portrayed the butler in Orson Welles' *The Magnificent Amberson's* (1942). He also played a porter in Orson Wells' WPA all-Black production of *Macbeth.*

Judy Cordova: She had been a vocalist with the John Kirby Sextet.

Millicent Roberts: She was a young dancer and beauty contest winner hired for the chorus.

Sidney Easton: He was an actor and songwriter who wrote, "Cast Away on an Island of Love," and who had also performed in minstrel shows, carnivals, Burlesque, and Vaudeville. He appeared in a number of movies, including *Murder on Lennox Avenue* (1941), and *Killer Diller* (1948).

Susie Sutton: She was an actress who had appeared on the *Death Valley Days* radio program, and was said to have been one of the best dramatic actresses at the time.
The Chanticleers
The Sepia Art Co-Eds
The Sepia Art Choir

I admire my father's idea of acknowledging the fact that he believed in providing specific entertainment for Black people, using Black people to do so. Eddie knew what it was like to work alongside Whites and he had no problems, to my knowledge, in doing so, but I am sure Eddie knew that if Blacks wanted to get ahead, they must help each other, by working together within their individual communities. I think Eddie might be saddened to see that today, the all-Black cast movie industry has not gotten as far as he may have hoped.

Eddie began to focus his energies on building his new film business by announcing a call for young women who were looking to be cast in a movie. A photo was printed in the *Pittsburgh Courier* of Eddie in his office interviewing five women who were placing applications. One of the women in the photo was Muriel Rahn. Muriel, though applying for movie work, had studied at the Julliard School of Music and would go on to become a leading Black concert singer, who was perhaps best-known for her starring role in the original Broadway production of *Carmen Jones* (1943). As mentioned earlier, Muriel was also the co-founder of the Rose McClendon Players, along with her husband, Dick Campbell. The couple were married until her death in 1961. Dick Campbell married for a second time, and with his wife, co-founded the Sickle Cell Disease Foundation of Greater New York. Dick died in 1994 at the age ninety-one.

Eddie took a small break during his foray into the movie business. In 1939, there was a program which was broadcast from September 29, 1935, until September 18, 1939 over the NBC Blue Network titled *The Magic Key of RCA,* an American variety radio show that featured an unusually large and broad range of entertainment stars and other noted personalities. A few of the stars to appear on this show were Paul Robeson, Fibber McGee and Molly, Tyrone Power, Ignacy Jan Paderewski, Walt Disney, Guy Lombardo, Eleanor Roosevelt, and on June 4, 1939, Eddie Green appeared along with the New Friends of Music String Quartet. *The Magic Key of RCA* was hosted by announcers Milton Cross (the same gentleman that introduced Eddie's comedic act to the television audiences back in July 1936), and Ben Grauer.

As a moviemaker, Eddie did it all: he wrote scripts and directed, starred in, and produced them. His first movie was a short titled *Dress Rehearsal* (1939), which featured "An All-star Colored Cast" that included him and Bonnie Marie Skeete. *Dress Rehearsal* was a movie short set in a well-attended, island-themed nightclub, with beautiful chorus girls providing entertainment, along with singers and various comedy skits. The plot may have been an expanded sound version of Eddie's 1916 silent movie, *Eddie Green's Rehearsal.* This new *Dress Rehearsal* was copyrighted September 23, 1939 as a 35mm, black and white film with sound, under Sepia-Art Pictures Co. Eight prints were placed on deposit.

I located a copy of the script at the Margaret Herrick Library in Beverly Hills, California, but the script consists of only eighteen pages of dialogue from Eddie's first three movies. Here is a small portion of what I believe is from *Dress Rehearsal:*

"This joint is jumping. Hey, Hey!"

Dress Rehearsal (1939).

FIRST MAN: What are you doing here? I wrote you a letter four days ago, didn't you get it?

SECOND MAN: Yes, here it is.

FIRST MAN: Well, can't you read, it says your services are no longer required, why did you come back?

SECOND MAN: Well, the envelope says "return in 5 days."

Dress Rehearsal proved to be quite popular, prompting Billy Rowe to refer to Eddie as the "comic movie making mogul." Mr. Frank Schiffman, co-owner of The Apollo, gave *Dress Rehearsal* high praise, after which he and Eddie discussed a purchasing deal.

In September, Eddie signed release papers with Jimmy Marshall, manager of The Apollo, and the movie had an early showing at the 125th Street Apollo on October 21, 1939. Leonard Harper, the producer of the 1923 play *Plantation Days* in which Eddie made an appearance, was now the in-house Apollo theater producer. He was also present at the signing.

Billy Rowe, one of the most influential journalists in the Black community during the 1930s-1950s, wrote the widely syndicated column, "Billy Rowe's Note Book," for the *Pittsburgh Courier* from 1935 to 1951. He also became New York's first Black Deputy Police Commissioner.

In October, Eddie sold his short, for showings in the South, to Mr. Rufus Byars, the Black general manager of the Lichtman chain of theaters in the South, which was founded by Abraham E. Lichtman. The circuit consisted of over thirty theatres at its height, all serving the Black community.

While Eddie's picture was showing, he never stood still. He was featured on the premier show of *The Pursuit of Happiness*, hosted by Burgess Meredith, on October 22, 1939, where he performed his "colored" version of "Christopher Columbus."

The Pursuit of Happiness, begun in 1939, was a series of programs, that, "for a little while will turn aside from the stream of grave events and bring us reminders that today, with thankfulness and humility, we Americans still enjoy our constitutional rights to life, liberty and the pursuit of happiness," according to Mr. W. B. Lewis, Vice-President in charge of broadcasts at CBS.

Later that year, a "first" occurred for Eddie in regard to his movie, *Dress Rehearsal:* it was telecast by the National Broadcasting Company (NBC). The *Pittsburgh Courier* printed on December 16, 1939, "History was made here Saturday afternoon, when the National Broadcasting Company picked the Sepia-Art Pictures Company's featurette, *Dress Rehearsal,* featuring Eddie Green, to broadcast over their television station here in New York City.

Not only is *Dress Rehearsal* the first Negro motion picture ever to be broadcast by television, it is, to its credit, written and produced in its entirety by Negroes. Eddie Green was the first Negro performer to appear on television. This first official broadcast took place July, 1936. Now Mr. Green again breaks a precedent by starring in the first film of its kind ever to be sent out over the air."

The New York Age printed basically the exact same article except for their title, "Nat'l Broadcasting Company Telecasts Eddie Green Film", and the fact that they printed the time of the broadcast, 2:30 p.m.

Because *Dress Rehearsal* was so well received, Sepia Art Pictures, which was then known as one of the few Black-owned motion picture-producing enterprises, had begun receiving letters from exhibitors demanding that the second picture be put out at once. Eddie's crew went into the production of another movie short right away.

What Goes Up, the new short, starred (who else) Eddie Green, Babe Matthews, Dick Campbell, "Honey Boy" Johnson, Sidney Easton, Carol Pertlow, Millicent Roberts, and the Sepia Art Choir, and had been released by April of 1940.

About a month before I finished this book, I was contacted by a woman named Sharon, who told me that her grandmother was Millicent Roberts, one of the cast members from *What Goes Up.* Sharon told me that her grandmother, who was then ninety-eight years old, had been telling the much younger family members for years that she had once worked in movies, and that she had also been a beauty contest winner. Because of her grandmother's advanced age, and the fact that the years she was talking about were so long ago, her stories "went in one ear and out the other." After hearing the stories "one more time," Sharon decided to conduct a little research, and in the process of searching historical newspapers, she discovered photos of her grandmother receiving her "Miss Glamorous" trophy on October 18, 1941, at the famous Renaissance Casino in New York.

Sharon also discovered a print of a poster from the movie, *What Goes Up,* which featured Eddie and a few of his chorus girls, one of which was Millicent. Her experience was that she went to a studio somewhere in New Jersey, where Eddie went over the chorus rehearsing schedule. Millicent was the chorus leader, and she said that she remembered reading her lines from a board. She played the part of "a little miss fresh mouth." She remembered being photographed in a bathing suit to promote the picture, and she said that the pictures were glamorous, "just like Hollywood photos." Millicent later saw the movie at The Apollo Theater.

In 1941, when Millicent won the "Miss Glamorous" contest in Harlem, Eddie took her to Bill Robinson's Mimo Club to celebrate. The Mimo Club, which had opened in February of 1941 at Seventh Avenue and 132nd Street, was a popular Harlem spot. The club featured an all-Black variety show, and was reported to be the place to visit when coming to Harlem. Millicent, after being introduced to the crowd as the new Miss Glamorous and receiving a standing ovation, spent the rest of that night accepting congratulations.

In regard to being re-discovered at the age of ninety-eight, Millicent said she was very happy, as she thought this had all been forgotten. She never imagined anyone would be talking about this more than seventy years later. On a recent doctor visit, her son showed her doctor a picture of Millicent from the movie, and Millicent said "everything stopped." The doctor and his staff made a big fuss over having a "celebrity" in their office, which made her very happy. Millicent said she was very happy that her granddaughter did

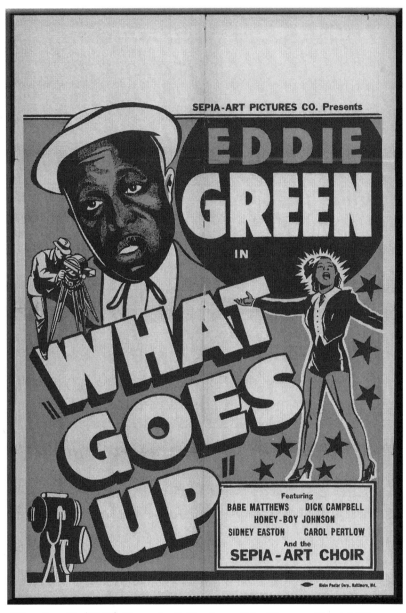

What Goes Up (1939). From the Collections of the Margaret Herrick Library.

the research and found her picture on a poster for *What Goes Up*, and that she would love to see the movie again.

A poster for *What Goes Up* is viewable at the Margaret Herrick Library in Beverly Hills, California, in the Edward Mapp Collection. The publisher of the poster was Globe Poster Corporation, in Baltimore, Maryland. As with the first "short" (an industry term meaning that the film is an original motion picture which has a running time of 40 minutes or less), the film may no longer exist.

During this time, Eddie began to work with Mr. Chauncey Northern, well-known tenor and voice coach. Mr. Northern joined Sepia Art Pictures to be the head of the Sepia Art music department and its singers. According to the article, "Sepia-Art Pictures expects great things to be accomplished by these young singers under the careful and comprehensive direction of Mr. Northern."

Chauncey Northern, whose studios were located in Carnegie Hall, was a graduate of the Julliard School of Music and was one of the first Black singers to perform opera on the Italian stage. He spent a number of years in Europe, until returning to the United States in 1937, where he established a vocal arts school. The fact that he came on to work with Eddie must have been a great boon for Eddie. Chauncey Northern taught voice until he died in Englewood, New Jersey, at the age of ninety-eight.

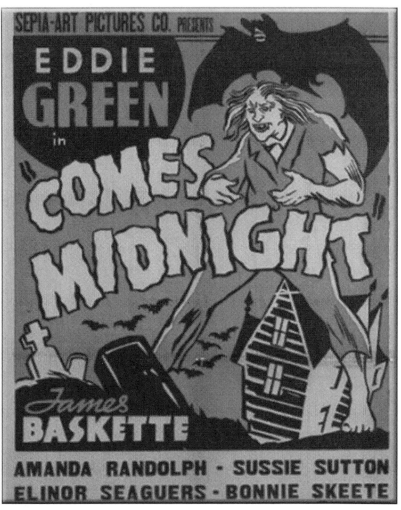

Comes Midnight (1940).

Chapter Thirteen

Rise of a Mogul

As was noted in the media, Eddie was making strides in realizing his ambition to become a businessman-producer. His first two movies, *Dress Rehearsal* and *What Goes Up,* were highly favored and touted as being real side-splitters. Eddie's films were seen as a new outlet for actors and actresses in Harlem.

By early 1940, work had begun on Eddie's third film, *Comes Midnight.* The cast included Eddie, Amanda Randolph, (who was at the time appearing on Broadway in *The Male Animal*), Susie Sutton, Elinor Seagures, "Honey Boy" Johnson, Bonnie Skeete, and James Baskette as the leading man.

Comes Midnight is a comedy about two men, played by Eddie and James, who will receive $100 if they stay in Old Man Mose's deserted house overnight, in order to dig up his body and get the gold that has been placed there. Amanda Randolph and Susie Sutton played the two spinsters that owned the house.

The house in which the movie was filmed was located in a New Jersey neighborhood. Eddie discovered that the neighborhood residents believed the house actually was haunted. According to them, groans had been heard coming from the house. After receiving this information, one of the original cast members refused to enter the house and was replaced by "Honey Boy" Johnson.

In May, *Comes Midnight* began showing at The Apollo Theater at 1530 Fulton Street in Brooklyn, with Mr. George Stamatis as manager. To give you an idea of the type of humor that was used in this movie, following are a few lines that Eddie actually used in a later skit for radio:

BASKETTE: Uncle Mose has a million dollars in gold ore.

GREEN: Gold or what?

In this next tidbit, the two are supposedly talking about skeletons moving about in the house, making noises, with one trying to scare the other:

BASKETTE: You hear rolling bones.

GREEN: I say "comes seven."

Today, these lines sound a little corny to me—corny but funny. The fact that I located the script for these movies, is what is most amazing. That someone took enough interest to take the time to collect and preserve items from these long-ago times, fosters the importance of Eddie's accomplishments and people like him, and provides me with a deeper appreciation of my father's life.

I have yet to discover any copies of *Comes Midnight,* perhaps, because what was then the Cocalis-Stamatis Circuit of theaters changed hands and became The Aldon Theatre Corporation, which then became the Columbia Amusement Company, Inc. With all that moving around, films could have been lost, thrown away, or sold. I have found that unless a film is definitely considered lost, it may still exist in someone's closet or museum. The *Comes Midnight* poster, published by the Globe Poster Corporation, can be viewed in the Margaret Herrick Library in Beverly Hills, California, in the Edward Mapp collection.

When searching for actresses to appear in his movies, Eddie found that beauty contests were a good venue for finding talented women. Carol Pertlow and Millicent Roberts, who appeared in *What Goes Up,* were two such ladies, as was Bonnie Skeete from *Comes Midnight*. Eddie would also become a major sponsor of one of the most anticipated beauty contests to be held at the 1940 World's Fair, the Miss Sepia America contest.

There appears to exist a filming of a compilation of Eddie's first three movies, titled *Eddie's Laugh Jamboree*, or *Eddie's Laff Jamboree* as it appeared in theaters in 1944, as a Ted Toddy production. From what I have come to understand, through viewing copies of sales transactions, Mr. Ted Toddy, a prominent White gentleman from Atlanta, Georgia, gained access to many All-Black cast films back in the 1940s.

Ted Toddy was what the papers of that time called a "pioneer" in the production and distribution of movies featuring an all-Black cast. He travelled from his base in Atlanta, specifically to obtain the films and begin production. He was the principle of Dixie Film Exchange, also known as Dixie National Pictures, Inc., in Atlanta, Georgia. He had offices in New York, Chicago, Dallas, and Hollywood. He became head of the Consolidated Film Exchange, with whom Eddie did business in 1941, per invoices I have found, which document the sale of negatives, prints, and stills, from Eddie to Consolidated. Perhaps, someday Eddie's films will resurface.

While Eddie was busy making his movies, a gentleman who had come along just ahead of him—Mr. Ralph Cooper—was busy becoming famous. He was a Black American movie producer and writer, and he was the originator of Amateur Night at The Apollo in 1935. He was also a big-time movie star. In 1940, he was the star attraction in the film, *Am I Guilty*, directed by Sam Newfield.

As part of Eddie's leisure hours away from the studio, on June 21, 1940, he attended the world premiere of *Am I Guilty*, the Hollywood produced All-Black film. This was a star-studded affair. Those in attendance included Mrs. Bill Robinson, Noble Sissle, and Mrs. Josephine Rowe.

Old newspaper articles from the 1940s show some of the other names that appear alongside Eddie's. For instance, Coleman Hawkins and his band appeared at the 125th Street Apollo, Ella Fitzgerald was on her way to Hollywood, Charlie Barnette and Jimmy Dorsey were in New York with the Count Basie band, and *Gone with the Wind* was playing at the Renaissance. Stepin Fetchit was in Johnstown experiencing what it was like to deal with "Jim Crow," and Paul Robeson was stopping the *Show Boat* in Angel City.

Following the success of Eddie's first three movies, a couple of in-depth articles were printed about him. One article titled "Meet Eddie Green" gave an overview of his life until 1940, mentioning his roots as a Baltimorean, and also mentioning his stint as KoKo in *Hot Mikado*. The article mentions, too, his barbecue stands in New York. The main point of the article was the fact that, as a writer and producer of "what many people believe are the finest films being released about our people," Eddie was a good business man.

In regard to the making of his movies, Eddie is quoted as saying, "The first thing I try for is naturalness. I write my own stories, building them around some incident that has been interesting, but not offensive. Then, I select the actors that I think are best suited to the parts, so that they need only be themselves. We usually rehearse for a short about two weeks."

In the article, Eddie states that the cameraman he uses most of the time is Don Malkames, a veteran when it comes to cameras, and Calvin Smith, a young man who was also attending the Institute of Photography in New York. It was noted that an important attribute in the making of any motion picture is an experienced cameraman, particularly in photographing Black actors, as "there is a wide variety of skin colors and tints to be found in the colored race."

Eddie told the interviewer that a typical day for him included going to the office, having lunch with his wife at home, and, if necessary, going to the recording studio. At night, after dinner, he liked to "tinker" with his ham radio, and later, he paid a visit to his barbecue places until midnight, went home, and would probably end his night signing-off from his shortwave station. When he was questioned about his recipe for success, he said, "The best recipe for success that he has, is to find something you like to do, and do that the best you know how."

The second article from *The New York Age* began with the caption, "Tells of Rise of Eddie Green and Sepia Art Pictures Company." This June 29, 1940 article was by Mary E. Finger, who spoke with Jack Caldwell, Sales Manager of Sepia Art Pictures Company. Sepia Art Picture's progress, according to Mr. Caldwell, ". . . was due to Eddie's prior radio experience, which had afforded him special passes to all the major studios, and that it was through this medium that Mr. Green's experience about operating such an institution is of inexhaustible strength for the future of this only Negro movie concern."

The interviewer was advised that "after the first showing of *Dress Rehearsal*, the White as well as the Negro audiences grabbed at it greedily. Due to this unexpected phenomenon, the entire plant had to be reorganized." According to Mr. Caldwell, "Mr. Green is the same man you see on the screen whether your association with him be social or business. The only difference you find is his keenness and his shrewd observation. He never misses a thing."

My guess is that Eddie never missed a chance to perform, either, as even though he was busy making movies, he was always available to appear on various radio programs. One of those programs was the *Tommy Riggs and Betty Lou* program. This popular show was a radio situation comedy broadcast from 1938 to 1946. Tommy Riggs switched back and forth from his baritone voice to the voice of a seven-year-old girl during his radio act, hence, Betty Lou, who was established as his niece. I believe this was a one-time appearance.

Eddie's next radio appearance was on April 28, 1940, on *The Jell-O Program* starring Jack Benny. The *Jell-O Program* originated out of the Ritz Theater in New York City, with Don Wilson, Phil Harris, Dennis Day, Mary Livingstone, Eddie Anderson (Rochester), and Charlie Cantor. Eddie's character in this sketch is Mr. DeWitt. Mr. Benny is quite upset with Rochester. He has Mary Livingstone call Rochester at the Theresa Hotel in New York. Mr. Dewitt answers the telephone:

MARY: Hello, Theresa Hotel, I'd like to speak to Rochester Van Jones, please.

JACK: Gimmie that phone. Hello?

MR. DEWITT: Hello.

JACK: Hello, Rochester?

MR. DEWITT: Just a minute, I'll see if he is unpreoccupied.

JACK: Unpreoccupied or not, I want to talk to him.

MR. DEWITT: Who shall I say is calling, please, in other words, who is you?

JACK: Who is I? Who is you?

MR. DEWITT: I'm Mr. Van Jones' secretary, Mr. DeWitt.

JACK: Well, I'm Mr. Benny, Rochester's boss, so put him on.

MR. DEWITT: Okay, Mr. Benny, okay. Get off his lap, Sugar, he's wanted on the phone.

The Broadway production of *Hot Mikado* ended with its last performance in June 1939, and Mike Todd had already moved the *Hot Mikado* production to the World's Fair in April. Believe it or not, during this period, Eddie was still performing in *Hot Mikado* at the World's Fair, said to be one of the most popular attractions, running through the second season until the fair closed on October 27, 1940.

Also, if, on Tuesday afternoon of July 30, 1940, one was still looking to be entertained by Eddie Green and you only had time for a good short movie, according to the Television column of *The New York Sun*, you could catch *Comes Midnight* at 3:55 p.m. that afternoon, right after the 3:48 p.m. film, *Tour of the World's Fair*, which makes this the second of Eddie's films to be shown on television.

Chapter Fourteen

The Mogul and the Beauty Contestants

O ne of the special exhibits at the New York World's Fair was the Miss Sepia Beauty Contest, where the winner would be crowned Miss Sepia America on August 15, 1940. Eddie, "Harlem's favorite Hollywood comedian," had been commissioned by the World's Fair to conduct a nationwide search for Miss Sepia America, and to be the guiding eye for the young ladies that would participate. One of Eddie's duties was to arrange various mini beauty contests around New York, in order to find ladies to participate in the contest at the World's Fair. The lucky winner of the Miss Sepia America contest would be starred in a picture with Sepia Art Pictures.

The St. Peter Claver R. C. Church was conducting their annual post-season Basketball Game and Matinee Dance presented by Alfred E. Duckett, in the church auditorium, and had requested that Eddie make an appearance with a few of the beauty contestants. Eddie consented and brought six of his contestants to the Claver affair, to give the Borough of Brooklyn a chance to meet the lovely contestants who had applied from various states. I am sure, this was probably one of the more pleasing aspects of Eddie's being of service to the World's Fair.

St. Peter Claver R. C. Church was the first African-American Catholic

Church in the Brooklyn diocese. The church was founded in 1921 by the Colored Catholic Club and Reverend Bernard Quinn. The church is now located at 29 Claver Place, Brooklyn, New York. On February 26, 1922, Bishop Thomas E. Molloy dedicated the impressively renovated church building and placed it under the patronage of St. Peter Claver, who was referred to as the Apostle of the Negroes. The mission of this group was that one day the "Colored" Catholics of Brooklyn would have their own pastor and their own parish church.

In the early part of August, Eddie sponsored a beauty contest at the Renaissance Club in New York. The affair, titled "Night of Glamour," was attended by newspaper and weekly publications reporters who served as judges. There were twenty-five young ladies, chosen for charm, personality, and a shapely figure. At the end of the competition, the audience chose Miss Rowena Smith as "Miss Glamour." A silver loving cup was presented to her by none other than Gypsy Rose Lee.

The winner of the Miss Sepia America beauty contest, however, was Miss South Carolina, Helen Lewis. According to the press, "Flash bulbs popped, cameras clicked, and thousands cheered in the World's Fair Court of Peace last Thursday night as glamour took a beating and sweet, unsophisticated innocence, personified by seventeen-year old Helen "Miss South Carolina" Lewis, was crowned "Miss Sepia America" in a battle of beauty staged by Eddie (Sepia Art Pictures) Green."

Miss Lewis had participated in an earlier contest, Miss Bronze America, conducted by the American Negro Association at the Chicago Coliseum. After she received her first prize honors for the "Miss Sepia America" contest, she was treated to a New York sight-seeing tour by Eddie, "master-mind behind the contest." Miss Lewis also received a movie contract with Sepia Art Pictures for a movie that would be released the next year.

The day after the beauty contest, Eddie celebrated forty-nine years of age by making an appearance at the Omega Showboat, sponsored by the Epsilon Chapter of the Omega Psi Phi Fraternity, joined by the Southennaires.

Ten days later, on August 26, 1940, Columbia Broadcast System aired *Forecast*, a series titled *"All God's Children."* If Columbia could get sponsorship for their program, they wanted to offer the series to their audience featuring "four of America's greatest stars," in a variety of programs. It was decided to begin by choosing Paul Robeson to head the musical production, with Eddie Green, the Eva Jessye Choir, and Amanda Randolph, with a musical score by Earl Robinson, who composed "Ballad for Americans."

"All God's Children" was to be built around stories of legendary heroes, which Columbia felt was best suited to Mr. Robeson's talents. The skits for these shows would be written by John Tucker Battle. Mr. Battle is the gentleman who wrote Eddie's scripts when he worked with Rudy Vallee, doing his "Heroes Wuz People" jokes. Mr. Robeson had starred on Broadway in a revival of *The Emperor Jones* (1924), starred in Oscar Micheaux's silent film, *Body and Soul* (1925), was seen in 1928 in a London Production of *Show Boat*, where he blew everyone away with his rendition of "Ole Man River." Mr. Robeson was also known for singing "Song of Freedom" and "King Solomon's Mine," among many other popular recordings. His career had reached an even higher plateau with the release of the film version of *The Emperor Jones* (1933), *Sanders of the River* (1935), *Song of Freedom* (1936), *Showboat* (1936), and *King Solomon's Mines* (1937).

Amanda Randolph had just recently appeared in Eddie's last movie, *Comes Midnight*. The Eva Jessye Choir was created by Eva Jessye, the first Black woman to receive international distinction as a professional choral conductor. She had also worked as musical director with George Gershwin on *Porgy and Bess* (1935).

A lot happened for Sepia Art Pictures Company in that first year, and on September 7, 1940, Eddie gave a luncheon for the Press in honor of the occasion, which was held at Gaylord's Blue Room in New York. Eddie, who, as one reviewer said, "has succeeded to the mantle of the late Bert Williams," was host to the Negro press, which included R. A. Melver and E. McGowan of the *Atlanta World*, Floyd Britt and Billy Rowe of the *Pittsburgh Courier*,

Major Robinson of the *Chicago Defender* and William E. Clark of the *New York Age*.

During the festivities, Eddie announced that he had a "full-length, all-Negro" feature going into production within the next three weeks and that the cast of the movie would include Helen Lewis, the winner of the Miss Sepia America beauty contest. Eddie was joined for the occasion by Mr. Jack Caldwell, Sepia Art Pictures Business Manager, Dewey Wineglass, Talent Scout and Production Manager.

Adding a little glamour, September 26, 1940 found Eddie and Hazel Scott appearing together in a dramatic skit on the WEBR radio program, *Bishop and the Gargoyle*. It was said that Eddie, the veteran comic, "provided some lusty laughs." Miss Scott, who was a well-known pianist/singer, in the switching of roles for one night, was said to show promise as an actress.

Born June 1920, Hazel Scott was given scholarships from the age of eight to study at the Juilliard School. She began performing in a jazz band in her teens, and was performing on radio at age sixteen. In 1950, she became the first Black woman to have her own TV show, *The Hazel Scott Show*.

On December 15, 1940, Eddie again appeared on *The Jell-O Program* starring Jack Benny, and one week later, on December 22, 1940, he was heard on the *Star Spangled Theater* in a program titled *Chester*.

Eddie was doing well by now, so well that he was able to play host to 250 needy people on Christmas Eve 1940, by treating them to Christmas baskets with roasted chicken and all the trimmings. He provided free tickets to a few of his friends, and these friends distributed the tickets to the people they felt were in the most need. The baskets were distributed from one of Eddie's two restaurants with Eddie, his manager, and his waitresses, doing the honors.

Chapter Fifteen

A New Venture—*Duffy's Tavern,*
The Radio Program

The active comedic course of Eddie's life would not be complete if it didn't include appearances out of the blue. *The Ben Bernie Music Quiz Show* featured "Comedian Eddie Green" in a show titled "Sweeny with the Dark Brown Wool." Apparently, the show was being renovated, and maybe they thought Eddie would jazz it up a bit. Probably, judging by the year, the title had to have been a play on "Jeannie with the Light Brown Hair." I don't know for sure, but I came across this information in the *Interlaken Review* from February 28, 1941.

In 1941, Eddie's roller coaster was climbing and getting closer and closer to the top. His popularity was growing due to his "Heroes Wuz People" skits, and also because of the fact that he became a regular on a new radio program, *Duffy's Tavern.*

Duffy's Tavern was the creation of Ed Gardner, who was born Edward Francis Poggenberg on June 29, 1901, in Astoria, Long Island. Before he created *Duffy's Tavern,* Ed held various jobs selling pianos, typewriters, and even paint. In 1929, he gave up his salesman career and began work in the entertainment industry. He became a theater producer with the Works Progress Administration (WPA), an actor in radio broadcasting, and went on to become a writer, director, and producer for J. Walter Thompson advertising agency. Sometime in 1938, the character of "Archie" was born. By July 1940, Ed had finalized his plans for *Duffy's Tavern* and he became "Archie."

Duffy's Tavern ran from March 1, 1941, through December 28, 1951. The theme song was "When Irish Eyes Are Smiling," written by Chauncey Olcott and George Graff, Jr. The regular *Duffy's Tavern* cast members were Ed Gardner as Archie, (the manager of the tavern, who had a "definite knack for handling malaproprisms"), Eddie Green as "Eddie, the waiter," (whose character's full name is Edward Pluribus Green), Shirley Booth (Ed Gardner's wife at the time) as Miss Duffy, Charles Cantor as Clifton Finnegan, and Alan Reed as Clancy the Cop.

Shirley Booth was born Marjory Ford in 1989 in Brooklyn, New York. She began her career onstage in 1925. Shirley appeared in *The Philadelphia Story* (1939). She won a Tony award in 1950 for *Come Back, Little Sheba*, appeared in *A Tree Grows in Brooklyn* (1951) and she won the Oscar in 1952 for Best Actress in a Leading Role for the movie version of *Come Back, Little Sheba*. What I found interesting and surprising was that she was the star of *Hazel*, a situation comedy I used to watch back in the 1960s. Shirley Booth passed away in 1992 at the age of ninety-four.

Mr. Charles (Charlie) Cantor was born on September 4, 1898. Beginning his career in 1921, he worked on such shows as *The Shadow* and *Dick Tracy*. He was so popular that sometimes he worked on forty shows a week. He also appeared on television in *Life of Riley* (1953), *Alfred Hitchcock Presents* (1955-1956), and the *Dick Van Dyke Show* (1963), to name a few. Charles Cantor passed away on September 11, 1966.

Alan Reed, born Theodore Bergman on August 20, 1907, was a radio actor performing in such shows as *The Life of Riley* and *The Shadow*, a stage actor who appeared in plays on Broadway, and he also provided voice-overs for movies and television characters, such as Fred Flintstone on Hanna Berbera's animated television show *The Flintstones* and *Pebbles and Bam-Bam*. Mr. Reed passed away June 14, 1977.

Once a week, *Duffy's Tavern* entertained America's citizens with the antics of Archie, the dubious responses of Eddie, the waiter, the man-chasing ideas of Miss Duffy, and the dim-witted conversation of Finnegan. The format of the show was to include a different guest celebrity each week, although that was not always the case. However, over the years, quite a few celebrities were in the tavern, such as, Bill "Bojangles" Robinson, Orson Welles, Milton Berle, Gloria Swanson, Tallulah Bankhead, Joe E. Brown, Frank Fay, Deems Taylor, Leo Durocher, Lucille Ball, Charles Laughton, Roy Rogers, Carmen Miranda, Lena Horne, Frank Sinatra, and so many more. There were two live broadcasts each week, one broadcast for the west coast and one for the east coast, with summer hiatus usually from June to October. The show began with the ringing of a telephone, which Archie would answer with, "Hello, *Duffy's Tavern*, where the elite meet to eat, Archie, the manager speakin', Duffy ain't here."

Duffy's Tavern proved popular enough for Paramount to present a movie version in 1945, with a cast featuring thirty-two of its biggest stars, and three of the radio program's regulars, Ed Gardner, Eddie, and Charlie Cantor.

Duffy's Tavern cast sharing a laugh. Circa 1942. Courtesy of Ed Gardner, Jr.

Eddie found his greatest fame on *Duffy's Tavern*. Martin Grams, Jr., in his book, *Duffy's Tavern, A History of Ed Gardner's Radio Program*, classifies Eddie's character as a foil for Ed Gardner's Archie, not in an excited way, but by taking a "more leisurely course in the subtle knifing of Archie." Others, like the *Chicago Defender*, saw his character as "coming to the rescue" of the bungling Archie. The character of Miss Duffy was a rather man-hungry blond. Finnegan was a somewhat dimwitted patron of the bar, and Clancy, the cop, played by Alan Reed, popped in from time to time.

Though *Duffy's Tavern* was a major commitment for Eddie, he continued to make appearances on other programs, such as *The Columbia Workshop*, where on April 27, 1941, he performed a sketch titled "Jason Was a Man," adapted from the legend of Jason and the Golden Fleece, but from a "Black" perspective.

The Columbia Workshop was initially set up to invite writers and artists to explore for the public, the experiential nature of radio techniques, which purpose, over time, evolved into their writers and artists using their ideas to place greater emphasis on good dramatic works, instead of concise technical explanations.

Another function for which Eddie was chosen to perform was the Harlem Children's Center midnight benefit on June 7, 1941. The benefit showcased various celebrities of the time. The lineup of entertainers also included Andy Kirk and his Orchestra, Noble Sissle, Lena Horne, Paul Robeson, Gene Krupa and a group called Cat's n The Fiddle. Per Marv Goldberg's *R&B Notebook*, The Cat's n The Fiddle, signature tune, "I Miss You So," became an established standard. The members of the group at the time of the benefit were Lloyd "Tiny" Grimes, Austin Powell, Ernie Price, and Chuck Barksdale. In January of that year the group had recorded a session which produced eight "sides," which included "I'll Always Love You Just the Same," "One is Never Too Old to Swing," and "Crawlin Blues," just to name a few. In the writing of this biography, I made it a point to look up Cat's n The Fiddle, and I discovered a prolific group whose popularity spanned a number of years.

On July 5, 1941, one month after Eddie's performance at the Harlem Children's Center, Noble Sissle, President of The Executive Board of the Negro Actors Guild of America, gave a dinner in honor of their Secretary, Edna Thomas, and their retiring Secretary, Fredi Washington. The attendees included members of the Board, Mrs. Noble Sissle, W. C. Handy, Dr. Channing E. Tobias, Mrs. Bill Robinson, and Eddie, who attended this particular function with his wife, Constance.

I see my father as a man who was always on the go, in the middle of the action, wherever that was, taking care of business, talking with those who could help spread the word of Eddie Green's comings and goings. People like Billy Rowe of the *Pittsburgh Courier*. Mr. Rowe would print bits and pieces of Eddie's doings, such as the fact that Eddie was considering taking his "show" down South. The show would feature the various winners of the Sepia America and Bronze beauty contests. Unfortunately, this plan did not come to fruition. Though I am not aware of the complete story, I know that at least one of the contestant's parents were not in favor of their daughter traveling through the South.

Even as Eddie was appearing regularly on *Duffy's Tavern*, considering a tour of the South, and performing at benefits, he had also been busy working on a new movie at his Palisades studio. *One Round Jones* was a movie about a nightclub owner, who comes up with the idea to offer $50 to anyone who can go "one round" with his mystery fighter. Of course, Eddie is the "mystery fighter." He brought Helen Lewis, the winner of the Miss Sepia Beauty Contest, to New York to be featured in this, his first full length movie. Ruth Nelson and Alan Drew (who, I believe, gave up the entertainment world for the police department) were also featured in the movie. By July 1941, *One Round Jones* was in the cutting room.

The poster for *One Round Jones* declares, "It's Hep," "It's Hot," It's a Sizzler." However, reviews do not seem to exist. I received a copy of the press sheet for *One Round Jones* from the University of Florida, Smathers Library. The press sheet was from Toddy Pictures Company, copyrighted in 1946.

One Round Jones (1941).

It features a cutout from the original poster, placed in the bottom left-hand corner, of a scantily clad woman, which was taken from the original *One Round Jones* poster. The original poster was a "Sepia Production" released by Consolidated National Film Exchanges. Toddy Pictures acquired articles from Consolidated and re-released them under Toddy Pictures Productions.

I suspect that after Eddie made this movie, he ran out of money, because *One Round Jones* was his last movie until 1949. Unfortunately, he also began to lose members of his cast roster to White producers paying higher salaries. At least one cast member from *What Goes Up* in 1939 bowed out of *Comes Midnight* in 1940, possibly due to being offered a part (and more money) in *Paradise in Harlem,* directed by Joseph Seiden of Seiden Sound Films. Babe Matthews, who had starred in *What Goes Up*, also appeared in *Paradise in Harlem.*

Black film makers had a difficult time making movies if they did not have large sums of money, so a lot of Black actors and moviemakers consolidated

Original poster *One Round Jones* (1941).

with their White counterparts, who did have the funds. This was the case with Ted Toddy, a top producer of "race" films. White filmmakers during these years were intent on getting into the "all-colored" film market. Eddie had worked with White film services companies, such as the Cinema Services Corporation, while developing his movies, but when it came to directing and producing, he was determined to relinquish this role to no one, and I believe this mind-set meant that he had to put his moviemaking ambitions on hold.

I have located office invoices and receipts to and from Mr. Seiden of

Cinema Services Corporation, with Mathilda Seiden as the guiding light, for services such as editing, cutting, and movieola rental. But Eddie did not, as far as I know, work with Mr. Seiden in the making of any movies at the Seiden Sound Films studio, in Fort Lee, New Jersey

Joe Seiden was a veteran newsreel photographer before getting into the moviemaking business. Joe became the nation's leading producer of Yiddish movies, including *My Son* (1939) and *Eli, Eli* (1940), and eventually he began making movies in English. He also directed a second "race" film, *Othello in Harlem* (1940).

In June 1941, Eddie was on a summer break from *Duffy's Tavern*. I imagine he took some time that summer to clear up the evidence of his presence in Fort Lee. His secretary at Sepia Art Pictures, Ismay Yearwood, took a leave of absence to prepare for her delivery from the stork, and Eddie's restaurant business was still going strong. I found his restaurant ad in a New York newspaper saying that Eddie Green's Bar-Bee-Q restaurant was always open and had the finest southern hospitality.

On October 12, Eddie and his comedic partner at the time, Gee Gee James, appeared on *The Jell-O Program* starring Jack Benny, with Don Wilson, Dennis Day, Mary Livingstone, Phil Harris, and Eddie "Rochester" Anderson. The official title of this show was "Columbus Day," in honor of the holiday. This week, Rochester needed $50 from Jack in a hurry, to pay off his dice debts, and he uses Eddie (who plays Columbus Smith) as the go-between. Jack and Rochester converse via telephone, and Gee Gee James is the telephone operator who won't get off the line because she just happens to be one of Rochester's girlfriends, and she is quite upset about Rochester's antics.

Before the telephone conversation, Jack is talking with Don when there is a knock on the door:

(Knock, knock, knock.)

BENNY: Come in.

COLUMBUS: Excuse me for intruding, Mr. Benny, but I got a note for you.

BENNY: I'm sorry, I'm busy right now, come back later.

COLUMBUS: I would advise you to take a quick gander at this communique.

BENNY: All right, what's the note, what does it say?

COLUMBUS: I'm only a carrier pigeon, we ain't much on reading.

BENNY: Oh, ok, let's have it.

MARY: Who's it from, Jack?

BENNY: Who do you think it's from? Rochester. Listen to this, dear boss, please give bearer, Mr. Columbus Smith, Columbus?

COLUMBUS: Yea, that's me.

BENNY: Oh.

MARY: Happy Anniversary.

Hilarious laughter from the audience.

Before the year was out, Eddie had to be in Los Angeles, and so he took his very first flight from New York to Los Angeles. One news article reported, "At every stop, Green noticed what looked like the same little red gasoline wagon being wheeled out to refuel the plane. On arriving in L.A., the hostess asked Green: "Wasn't the trip wonderful? We almost made it in record time." "Yeah," countered the comedian, "and that little red truck didn't do so bad, either!"

Over the next few years, Eddie was back and forth from New York to Los Angeles. On one of these trips, Eddie met my mother, Norma Amato, for the first time. The meeting took place at Clifton's Cafeteria, which was located in downtown Los Angeles on Broadway. In those days, Clifton's was "the place to be" if one wanted to be seen. At the time, Clifton's had a waterfall upstairs, and mom and her mother, Sinclaire, sat by the waterfall. Sinclaire was a prominent citizen in Los Angeles and she liked to be seen as such. My mom told me that one day while she and her mother were having lunch at Clifton's, Eddie climbed the steps, walked to their table, and introduced himself. After some discussion, the trio discovered that Sinclaire and Eddie were acquainted with a few of the same people. One of these people was Hattie McDaniel, whom Eddie had met on a few radio programs and who he had also seen during his audition for *Gone with the Wind.* Turns out that Hattie McDaniel and Sinclaire were quite close. Over time, Eddie would become a part of this friendship, and Eddie and Hattie would also find themselves appearing together in various radio programs.

Chapter Sixteen
Can He Get Any Busier?

Febuary 20, 1942, the cast of the stage play, *My Sister Eileen*, starring Shirley Booth, gave a party to celebrate their 500th performance. The cast, including Miss Booth, put on a show called "Strictly for Laughs" in which Paul Draper, Benny Baker, Keenan Wynn, Eddie Green, and Ed Gardner appeared, according to the *New York Post*.

A section of the *New York Post* called "Plays and Players to Be Seen at Central Queens Theatres This Week" promoted Edward G. Robinson in *Unholy Partners* at the Savoy, Bing Crosby and Mary Martin in *The Birth of the Blues* at the Hillside Willard, John Payne and Claudette Colbert in *Remember the Day* at the Jamaica Queens, and Laird Cregar and Victor Mature in *I Wake Up Screaming*. Down in the corner of this page was Cagney in *Captain of the Clouds*, and on the right was Bette Davis and Monte Wooley in *The Man Who Came to Dinner*.

My father's name was on the same page as these other celebrities. He was coming along with people who were eventually considered the greats of their time, and he was one of those people. Later in the year, Mary Martin appeared on *Duffy's Tavern*.

By April 1942, America was embroiled in WWII, the government decided to draft "men of a certain age," not to fight necessarily, but to be available if needed. So, on April 7, 1942, Eddie reported to his draft board and signed up.

Cast of *Duffy's Tavern* with: Ed Gardner, Eddie Green, Shirley Booth, Charles Cantor, Dan Seymour, and Mary Martin. Photo courtesy of Ed Gardner, Jr.

The draft card asked for the name of a person who would always know the draftees' whereabouts, and Eddie listed his employer, William J. McCaffrey, whom, I discovered later, was also Clark Gable's agent. Eddie listed McCaffrey's address as 501 Madison Avenue, New York. This little card was a fount of information, as Eddie had to list his proper birthdate, which was August 16, 1891 (he had told others, including my mom, that it was 1896.) And it corroborated his business address at the time as being 2352 7th Avenue, New York.

Eddie was not called on to participate in any engagements during WWII. However, the entertainment industry itself was working to provide a sense of hope by putting on various benefits, and Eddie was always ready to be of service in that area. One of the benefits that year was for the Little Flower House of Providence for Homeless Colored Children in Wading River, Long Island, put on by the St. Peter Claver R. C. Church in Brooklyn. The population had grown at the St. Peter Claver Parish, and Rev. Quinn noticed there was a need for an orphanage for Black children. To address that need, he purchased the Oliver Paine Farm in Wading River, Long Island and converted it into an orphanage. The Little Flower House of Providence for Homeless Colored Children was established in Wading River. The orphanage was dedicated on October 30, 1930. Among the featured stars at this 1942 fall affair were Steppin Fetchit (my mom said they used to call him "High Steppin Fetchit"), The Mullen Sisters of the *Kate Smith Hour*, Pee Wee Marquette from the *Savoy Ballroom*, Ella Fitzgerald, Eddie, and the Savoy Sultans.

Running a restaurant, making appearances, and attending parties, was not enough for Eddie, especially when he was on summer hiatus from *Duffy's Tavern*. He had been considering opening some type of entertainment school for a couple of years and, in September 1942, after months of preparation, he opened a Musician's School at his place of business in New York. The school was a dramatic training school with services and classes for both amateurs and professionals. The school was named "Sepia Artists." Eddie was now fifty-one years old.

Between the time Eddie opened his Musician's School in September and the Christmas Holiday season, Eddie was showcased, along with Pinky Lee and the Delta Rhythm Boys, on *The Columbia Workshop* radio show in a special four-part program titled, "All Out for Comedy." The first of the four programs was "The Old-Fashioned Vaudeville Show."

With Christmas approaching, people were looking for ways to lighten the mood of the country, so the Columbia Network's radio show, *Caravan*, decided to provide an hour of fun and music, "with a veritable blitz on gloom," by providing to its audience a night of fun instead of their usual dramatic fare. Soldiers were polled and it was discovered that the majority—eighty-seven percent—preferred popular music, while eighty-five percent preferred comedy. Eddie was asked to "bring back some of his famous fables," to help entertain the troops.

In order to boost the morale of the nation's soldiers, the War Department, on May 26, 1942, created a division of men called the Armed Forces Radio Service (AFRS). The AFRS began recording the *Jubilee* radio program. The show was directed at Black Troops, but the high quality jazz was enjoyed by all of those in service. The program stated that it was for the Fighting Men of the United Nations.

Initially, AFRS programming included mostly transcribed, commercial network radio shows, such as the *Kraft Music Hall*. Soon, numerous original AFRS programs, such as *Mail Call*, were added to the mix. Lt. Col. Thomas A.H. Lewis (Commander of the Armed Forces Radio Service) wrote in 1944, "The initial production of the Armed Forces Radio Service was *Mail Call*, a morale-building half hour, which brought famed performers to the microphone to sing and gag in the best American manner." At its peak in 1945, the AFRS was generating about twenty hours of original programming each week. The AFRS could command the services of the best writers and performers, without regard to their network or studio contractual obligations.

Early episodes of another AFRS show, *Jubilee*, were emceed by Dooley Wilson, (the actor who portrayed Rick's piano player in *Casablanca*), but most episodes were hosted by Ernest Whitman. Musical guests included Lena Horne, Louis Armstrong, Scatman Carruthers and His Orchestra, Duke Ellington, Count Basie, the Teddie Wilson Sextet, The Mills Brothers, "Fats" Waller, Bing Crosby, Kay Starr, Stan Kenton, and Les Paul.

Eddie's first *Jubilee* program was December 25, 1942, with Ernest Whitman as emcee ("Thank Youuu, thank youuu!" was his catch phrase). The show featured The Count Basie Orchestra, The Delta Rhythm Boys, Lena Horne, and Bing Crosby. Lena Horne, Eddie, and Ernest Whitman, presented a comedy routine titled "Christmas Present." Eddie was the person who received the present, and Lena was the present. Ernest Whitman was Santa Clause. Also, Lena sang "Silent Night," and Bing Crosby sang "Gotta Be This or That."

I present to you a portion of "Christmas Present":

SANTA: Boy, boy, have I got a present for some G. I. guy. I've got Lena Horne all wrapped up, and I'm gonna deliver her to some lonesome PFC overseas. Will he be surprised!

Announcer: It's the night before Christmas, the whole camp's asleep and here comes Santa Claus, jivin' in his Jeep. But wait, it's not as quiet as it would seem, awake in his tent is Pfc. Eddie Green!

EDDIE: Oh me, it's Christmas. Not even a fire place. Oh well, I'll hang my stocking on the tent pole. Maybe somebody will drop about 50 points in it. I remember when my mother put an orange in my stocking. For a whole week I walked with a squish. You know, if I really believe in Santa Claus, I'd get that bicycle what I want, with a saddle seat.

Bells jingling.

EDDIE: Well I'll be durn, that's either sleigh bells or the cook is banging those Spam cans again.

Soldiers laughing.

SANTA: Hello, hello, hello!

EDDIE: Well, what chu know, it's Santa Clause.

SANTA: What would you like for Christmas?

EDDIE: Just what every soldier would like sittin' right down on his lap.

SANTA: And what would every soldier want sittin' right down on his lap?

EDDIE: Something round and fluffy, kinda curved, and something very sweet.

SANTA: You mean?

EDDIE: Angel food cake.

SANTA: Well, my boy, I brought you something that you'll like. This is your package.

EDDIE: Now that is good. Mmmmm. Some package there, and so nicely wrapped.

SANTA: And now, you musn't open it until Christmas morning.

EDDIE: No huh, I can't even loosen the wrapper?

SANTA: No, no. If you do I'll come back and get it.

(Santa leaves.)

EDDIE: That's a swell looking bundle. I wonder if it . . . it's big enough to be a bicycle. That could be the round fenders, there.

(Laughter from the audience.)

EDDIE: I guess I'll open it. Well, looka here, it's a Lena Horne mama's doll, ain't that nice. It'll be good if when I squeeze it, it says mama.

LENA: Oh daddy.

EDDIE: Well, that's good enough.

LENA: Eddie, put your arms around me. Hold me tight. Kiss me.

EDDIE: This is a talking doll with ideas.

LENA: Come on, come on, kiss me.

EDDIE: This is a persistent doll, too. Ok, now. (SMACK.) Man, what they can do with sawdust nowadays.

LENA: Eddie, Eddie, I'm not a doll. I'm really Lena Horne.

EDDIE: No, I can't believe that. Santa Clause dropping Lena Horne right here in my lap?

LENA: Isn't this just the nicest Christmas you ever had?

EDDIE: Naw, last year we had a tree.

[Thanks to two friendly people, who were closing their business and just happened to have copies of live excerpts of *Jubilee* programs, I have this show on a CD. It's so funny listening to Lena Horne saying, "Oh daddy" in that sexy voice, to my father. I know it was just an act, but, after all, Lena was a doll.]

Lena Horne began her show business career in 1932 at the age of six-teen. She appeared in numerous movies, including *The Duke is Tops (1938)* with Ralph Cooper, *Cabin in the Sky* (1943) with Ethel Waters, and *Stormy Weather* (1943) with Bill Robinson. Referred to as the "dusky beauty," her sultry singing voice helped propel her to stardom. By the 1990s, she had recorded over twenty albums. She appeared in guest spots on television, in-cluding *Sanford and Son.* She won two Tony Awards and numerous Grammy Awards. Lena Horne passed away on May 2, 2010.

Thanks to *Radiogoldindex*, it is possible to listen to some of the other old time radio shows in which Eddie appeared, one of which was the CBS-sponsored *Stage Door Canteen*, put on for the benefit of the nation's soldiers. On the December 3, 1942 show, Eddie joined host Bert Lytell, Connie Bo-swell, Louella Parsons, Robert Benchley, Raymond Paige and His Orches-tra, and the Benny Goodman Sextet. Connie Boswell opened the program with "Why Don't You Fall in Love with Me?" After Miss Boswell, Eddie, as a "busboy", and Robert Benchley, a "soldier," engage in a back and forth dialogue regarding Eddie doing "something important" for the war effort:

EDDIE: You know, soldier, looka here, I'd like to do something important in this war.

The soldier suggests Eddie fight the enemy via submarine.

EDDIE: Submarine?

SOLDIER: Yeah, you know, those boats that dive down under the water.

EDDIE: Oh no, not me. I'm stayin' on terra firma, and the more firma, the less terra.

In Hollywood, where people were feeling the stress of a "world at war," a special recording by Bing Crosby of "Silent Night" was made with "the Music Maids and John Scott Trotter's orchestra for the Coordinator of Inter-American Affairs at NBC's Hollywood Radio City for transmission to the Latin American neighbors."

Eddie was now fifty-one years old, though he only admitted to forty-six. The roller coaster of his life made it to that first pinnacle of its ride and was now preparing for its descent. It usually took a long time to get to the top and the first descent was a doozy. Not knowing much about life with Eddie personally, I can only speculate that because of events that occurred in the next few weeks, Eddie may have been experiencing some difficulties.

Even though life as an actor was proving busy, I am not sure how profitable it was for Eddie. At the beginning of the year, he filed for bankruptcy. He no longer had his restaurants or his movie-producing company. In his voluntary petition, he listed liabilities of $5,119 and assets of $473. He owed the government $445. The information was public knowledge, evidently. A *Pittsburgh Courier* columnist who thought of Eddie as a "fine fellow" observed that his misfortune "is not without sadness."

I imagine Eddie may have been a wee bit sad, but with the knowledge I have of him as a person, I do not see him as someone who would wallow in his misfortune. From what I have learned while researching this book, and according to my mom, he was usually upbeat, and always had something cooking. He had talent, drive, and ambition, and he was still a regular on *Duffy's Tavern*.

Thankfully, Eddie's role on *Duffy's Tavern* provided a continual source of income, as celebrities who performed at benefits did not receive a salary, and all appearances for *Jubilee* were donated by the performers for the benefit of the armed services. For a short time, beginning with season three, the word "Tavern" was dropped from the title of the show, due to the fact that some more sensitive folks objected to the word because it seemed to promote excessive drinking. The change was short-lived, however, and by March 1944, "Tavern" was restored to the title.

Speaking of *Duffy's*, after listening to the January 5, 1943 episode, I have the impression that Eddie may have assuaged his bad feelings through his comedy. Archie is having his usual nightly telephone call with Duffy. After informing Duffy that Mr. Milton Berle would be the guest for that evening, Archie returns to the sign that he was in the process of making before the call. Eddie walks in:

EDDIE: What's that, a sign to welcome Mr. Berle?

Archie explains that he is hanging a sign in regard to his New Year's resolution to follow the Golden Rule.

EDDIE: How about hanging up a sign for the waiter, me?

ARCHIE: Yea?

EDDIE: Yea, it could go something like this, "The Golden Rule has a fine intent, but a 10 cent tip will pay the rent.

Later that month, Eddie agreed to provide his comedic talent to the January 15, 1943 *Jubilee* program, this time starring saxophonist and band leader Jimmy Lunceford, jazz vocalist Maxine Sullivan, The Charioteers Gospel group, and Canada Lee, (an actor who, later that year, took a lead role as a Black man who had reservations about fighting the Japanese in the production of *South Pacific* directed by Lee Strasberg). Eddie and Canada Lee performed "Boxing," a comedy routine written by Eddie. Hattie McDaniel acted as Mistress of Ceremony. The following is a portion of the sketch that caused me to laugh out loud:

MISS McDANIEL: The clock says it's laughing time. And when it's time to laugh, then it's time to listen to Eddie Green and Canada Lee!

CANADA LEE: Remember some time ago, Eddie, I told you, that I think you would make a good prize fighter?

EDDIE: (laughingly) Yeah, I member that, I do.

CANADA LEE: Yeah, I can see the whole thing.

EDDIE: You can. Just a minute, who is I'm fighting?

CANADA LEE: Why, you're fighting Joe Louis.

EDDIE: No, I ain't, either. I bet I ain't.!

CANADA LEE: Oh yes you are. It's too late to back out now, Eddie. The bell rings for the first round. Louis leaps into the ring like a tiger.

EDDIE: And I leap out like another tiger.

CANADA LEE: No, no Eddie, you stand right up to him, and whoop, Louis just misses you with a terrific left, and what do you do?

EDDIE: I pray.

CANADA LEE: No, look. Now Louis, he makes a feint to his left and hits you right in the jaw.

EDDIE: Then I faint.

CANADA LEE: No, you back away. But are you discouraged?

EDDIE: Yes, I am.

CANADA LEE: No you ain't, you come back for more.

EDDIE: You crazy? I'm satisfied with what I got. Let me ask you something. When do I hit him?

CANADA LEE: Right now. You lead with your face and you hit him bang on the glove.

LONG PAUSE.

EDDIE: With my face? I bet that hurt him.

CANADA LEE: Now, Eddie, you've got Louis mad.

EDDIE: Yeah, I was afraid of that.

CANADA LEE: Now he comes at you with murder in his heart. Anybody else would run away, but not you.

EDDIE: What's the matter with me, am I glued to the floor?

In the meantime, season three of *Duffy's Tavern* having begun October 6, 1942, ended the run of thirty-nine broadcasts on June 29, 1943, leaving Eddie free to appear at a Benefit Carnival for Women in Uniform, at the Renaissance Casino on 138th Street and Seventh Avenue. The benefit was held to raise funds for the war effort. Among the stars who appeared were "Eddie Green, of *Duffy's Tavern*," and Ed Small's Paradise Revue. Don Wilson and his band provided the dance music.

Following this appearance, Eddie was listed in the *New York Post* as being a guest on the July 6 1943 *Meet the Colonel* program. *Meet the Colonel* was a radio show starring F. Chase Taylor as "The Colonel."

Frederick Chase Taylor was born on October 4, 1897, in Buffalo, New York. He broke into radio in 1924, and eventually became known as the character, Colonel Lemuel Q. Stoopnagle. Colonel Stoopnagle ran a bowling alley, with the help of Eddie, as his co-star. Mr. Taylor appeared as a guest performer many times on *Duffy's Tavern*, beginning with the first March 1941 episode.

Chapter Seventeen

Down Don't Mean Out

In early July 1943, fortune smiled on Eddie. Paramount Pictures decided to make the *Duffy's Tavern* radio program into a movie. Paramount used every major star they had on contract in this movie, and, as the radio program was the brain-child of Ed Gardner, he was also the star. Paramount decided that it was only natural that Mr. Gardner would appear in the movie version. Likewise, Charles Cantor, was signed on as his radio character, "Finnegan," and Eddie was signed on to play his character, "Eddie the waiter."

On July 19, 1943, *The Miami News* reported that Eddie had been signed to the *Duffy's Tavern* movie by producer Jack Moss. Here was a much needed boost to Eddie's psyche, I am sure. Although Eddie, as a movie producer himself, had bottomed out in that area, he was now going to be featured in a Hollywood-produced movie, among a cast of major celebrities. Filming started September 1944. He was now back in the money.

The October 19, 1943 *Duffy's Tavern* radio show guest was Peter Lorre. This episode was funny, with Mr. Lorre's gruesome ideas for what makes a good show, and the antics of Raffles, the talking Mynah Bird.

EDDIE: Hey, Mr. Archie, this talking bird, what do they call it?

ARCHIE: They call it a Mynah bird.

EDDIE: Why do they call it a Mynah bird?

ARCHIE: Look Eddie, I never talk on a subject of which I am ignorant.

EDDIE: Now that quiet nobody could be. Tell me, why do they call it a mynah bird?

ARCHIE: Cause it's a bird that ain't twenty-one years old.

ARCHIE: Don't forget, Eddie, for a long time, I was associated with the Explorer's Club

EDDIE: As a busboy.

ARCHIE: Maître d'water, they called me. Naturally, working in the Explorer's Club, it makes one practically an explorer oneself.

EDDIE: I was a waiter at the Stork Club for two years. I ain't never had a baby!

The cast of *Duffy's Tavern* saw a change this season as Florence Halop became the new Miss Duffy, due to Shirley Booth's decision to make a career change. Florence would portray Miss Duffy through March of 1944.

On December 10, 1943, four years after Eddie's first movie, *Dress Rehearsal,* premiered in New York, it was shown along with an Edward G. Robinson movie, *Destroyer,* at the Vogue Theater in Pittsburgh. Maybe that was because word got out that Eddie had been signed to the *Duffy's Tavern* movie. Whether Eddie was receiving royalties from the showing of his movie is a mystery to me.

The Radio Hall of Fame program on Sunday evenings presented itself as a weekly tribute to the best entertainment then available on stage, in radio, on recordings, and in motion pictures. To determine which performers and productions were worthy of recognition, the producers formed an alliance with *Variety,* the weekly "Bible" of show business, which closely followed events on all of the entertainment fronts. *Variety's* editors decided who and what deserved to be singled out in a given week. Basically, they decided which singers, actors, performers, stage productions, and films were garnering the most critical praise, and *Variety* would then recommend the line-up.

The *Radio Hall of Fame* was extremely successful in bringing the top entertainers into the homes of their listeners for two years. On January 30, 1944, Eddie appeared on the show along with Victor Herbert, Ed Gardner, and Bud Hulick. Ed Gardner told the story of "Two Top Gruskin," and Eddie and Bud Hulick performed a Minsky's Burlesque sketch, "Western Union."

The airwaves were still carrying programs to the nation's armed forces, and in April 1944, an AFRS presentation of *Mail Call* broadcast an English drawing room drama titled, *A Tribute to Brooklyn.* The cast in this drama included, Ed Gardner, Ida Lupino, Charles Cantor, and Eddie Green.

May 1, 1944 *Jubilee* showcased Eddie, Lena Horne, Jimmie Baskette, the Charioteers, and the Fletcher Henderson Orchestra. Eddie and Jimmie Baskette provided the laughs with "Haunted House," a skit that I believe was taken from Eddie's 1939 movie, *Comes Midnight.* Lena Horne sang "Honeysuckle Rose" and "Mad About the Boy."

On May 5, 1944, Eddie appeared again on *Jubilee.* The program begins with the announcer calling: "Hi Diddle, diddle, some cats bought a fiddle and went out on a spree, they play hot and sweet, gut bucket and heat, gentlemen, it's Jubilee! Rise and Shine all you hermits of the Hep, and sisters of the solid. Hot Horn Hall welcomes you with both valves wide open." Man, those cats were swinging.

This program stars Bob Parish, Dorothy Donnegan, and The Sweethearts of Rhythm. Ernest Whitman is the emcee, referred to as Ernie (Bubbles) Whitman on this show. Eddie and Ernie perform a comedy skit that has to do with Eddie getting a job. The following is a short version of the skit:

ERNIE: Have you any political inclination?

EDDIE: No, I leans over like this 'cause I've been sick, that's all.

ERNIE: Are you working?

EDDIE: No, I ain't workin'.

ERNIE: How old are you?

EDDIE: Thirty-nine years old.

ERNIE: How long have you been out of work?

EDDIE: Thirty-nine years.

The summer of 1944, Lena Horne hosted a press party after an appearance at the Orpheum Theater in Los Angeles, at which she served a lavish buffet. Invited guests included Rex Ingram and the gospel group The Charioteers. Among the guests that she introduced and invited to the stage was "that side-splitting comedian, Eddie Green."

Progress was being made, meanwhile, with the *Duffy's Tavern* movie. The tavern was being created, and Bob Hope, William Bendix, and Victor Mature had been cast, according to the *New York Sun*, July 31, 1944. In a September 6, 1944 article in the *Brooklyn Eagle*, it was reported that Bing Crosby was set to appear, along with Dorothy Lamour, Betty Hutton, and Ray Milland. It had been decided that Ed Gardner, Charles Cantor, and Eddie would be directed by Sidney Landfield, and Hal Walker would direct the film.

Meanwhile, season four of the *Duffy's Tavern* radio program ended after approximately thirty-eight episodes with their June 27, 1944 show, which was a special rebroadcast for the armed forces. Following is a short section:

Archie is anticipating being hired for the summer by a show called the *Nitwit Circuit*, and he and Eddie have a short discussion. This sketch gives you an idea of Archie's troubles with certain words and Eddie's greater ability to speak proper English, and also gives an idea of the "subtle knifing" of Ed Gardner's character, Archie, by Eddie, the waiter:

ARCHIE: Ransom Sherman has a new radio show, and there is a highly remote possibility that he might hire me.

EDDIE: Yea, but, you ain't no radio actor.

ARCHIE: There are two schools of thought on that, Eddie.

EDDIE: But, you never went to either one of them schools.

ARCHIE: Well, Eddie, it don't take no brains to be a radio actor.

EDDIE: That's why you so confident.

ARCHIE: Sure. That's the difference between you and me, Eddie, you know. We both got talent, where we dissemi . . . (Archie has trouble pronouncing the word)) . . . uh, I got confidence and you ain't.

EDDIE: No, no. Where we disseminate is, you say, you got talent and you got confidence, I say, I ain't got talent, I got confidence that you ain't got talent. What kind of radio program is this, anyhow?

ARCHIE: Why, it is called, the *Nitwit Court.*

EDDIE: Oh. You've got that one.

Beginning in about August, due to the fact that Eddie was now rehearsing for the *Duffy's Tavern* movie, he was restricted in how many venues he could perform. He could appear on other radio broadcasts one day a week, if he submitted not less than one week's prior written notice. This was probably a good thing, because *Duffy's Tavern* was moving from New York to Hollywood, and Eddie needed time to find a place to live.

By September, Eddie had moved to Los Angeles and taken up temporary residence with one of his friends, Miss Louise Beavers, until he could find a home. Miss Beavers was an actress who found fame in the movie, *Imitation of Life*, among other films, and who was living in what was then known as the "Sugar Hill" area of Los Angeles. Sugar Hill was the one place in Los Angeles where Blacks who had money could buy a home.

Eddie was fifty-two years old when he moved to Los Angeles, footloose and fancy-free, no longer married to the third Mrs. Green, but he did not intend to remain single. After an interview with him, Mrs. J. T. Gipson of the

Los Angeles California Eagle, reported, "Eddie (*Duffy's Tavern*) Green is ready to settle down and tie the knot. He has bought the home and he's just waiting for the right lovely to come along."

Season five of *Duffy's Tavern* began its broadcast from Hollywood on September 15, 1944, with Rudy Vallee as the guest. During the telephone conversation that Archie has with Duffy at the beginning of the show, Archie is trying to get Duffy to remember Rudy Vallee. So Archie, while holding his nose, begins to sing in a voice that he thinks sounds like Mr. Vallee. It was hilarious. The scene in the tavern begins with Archie and Eddie having a conversation:

ARCHIE: Here we are.

EDDIE: Here we are.

ARCHIE: You and me.

EDDIE: You and me.

ARCHIE: Back at Duffy's.

EDDIE: Back at Duffy's.

ARCHIE: Great feeling ain't it.

EDDIE: Stop the train, I'm gettin' off.

ARCHIE: Now, that ain't nice, Eddie. *Duffy's Tavern* is like our home, we should cherish it, love it, and Duffy too, you know, a guy who picked us up out the gutter and brought us here.

EDDIE: Mr. Archie, from the gutter to *Duffy's Tavern,* is not up.

(The audience laughs, but also breaths a collective sound of disapproval of the remark.)

ARCHIE: Eddie, what are you kickin' about? What's your salary now?

EDDIE: Same as last year, nothin'.

ARCHIE: Well, what do your tips come to?

EDDIE: A little less than the salary.

ARCHIE: How can your tips come to less than nothin'?

EDDIE: Very simple, several of our customers is pick-pockets.

Eddie, allowed time off from his Paramount activities to "render services" to radio broadcasts, did just that in October. The *Jubilee* radio show put on another broadcast from Hot Horn Hall, in Hollywood, California. This time, the show featured Erskine Hawkins and his Orchestra, Effie Smith, Eddie South, Leadbelly, Ernest Whitman, and Eddie.

Eddie and Ernest perform a hilarious routine, "Volunteer Fireman." Ernie introduces Eddie Green from *Duffy's Tavern*. Eddie says he is bored and is looking for something exciting to do in his life. Ernie suggests Eddie become a volunteer fireman:

ERNIE: It's Saturday morning at the station house and the alarm goes off. I can see you now, sound asleep up there in the firehouse.

EDDIE: So far, I like it.

ERNIE: Four in the morning the fire alarm rings, what do you do?

EDDIE: I get up. Then I take a sleeping pill and go right back to bed.

ERNIE: No, you don't. You grab your fire hat, run to the pole and slide down.

EDDIE: OOOO!!

ERNIE: What's the matter?

EDDIE: The pole is cold, I forgot my pants!!

The local paper advertised *Eddie's Laff Jamboree* showing at The Vogue alongside, *Algiers* starring Hedy Lamarr and Charles Boyer. *Eddie's Laff Jamboree* was a compilation of his first three movies, *Dress Rehearsal, What Goes Up,* and *Comes Midnight.* This movie was not produced by Eddie, but by another movie producer, possibly, after purchasing these "all-colored-cast" films from other production companies.

In November, back at the *Duffy's Tavern* radio program, there was a slight change at the beginning of the November 10, 1944 episode. Eddie, the waiter, answered the telephone.

Telephone rings.

EDDIE: Hello, *Duffy's Tavern,* Eddie, the head waiter speakin'. Say what? Reservation?

(He lets out a sort of high-pitched, incredulous giggle.) You know, you see mister, we don't make reservations here. Just come on down. If you find a chair that ain't busted, it's yours.

Life seemed to be going well for Eddie, what with the movie contract and his radio commitments, but the reality was that some things did not turn out well. Seems that he had made the decision to "unload" his string of restaurants, to his "post war" regrets.

Chapter Eighteen

Ed Gardner's
Duffy's Tavern, The Movie

January 1945 began with Eddie working with Mr. Boris Karloff on *Duffy's Tavern*. Eddie is the first person to greet Mr. Karloff when he arrives at the tavern:

EDDIE: Good evening, Mr. Karloff.

KARLOFF: You know, young man, you are refreshing.

EDDIE: What?

KARLOFF: Usually, when I walk into a place, they all act scared of me.

EDDIE: Oh. Well, you see, Mr. Karloff, when a man has worked at *Duffy's Tavern* for ten years, the only thing that can horrify him is another ten years.

After performing with Mr. Karloff, what could be better than going on to appear with Mr. Bob Hope on *The Radio Hall of Fame*. The program originated from The Earl Carroll Theatre Restaurant in Hollywood. Bob Hope served as the emcee. Paul Whiteman and his Orchestra provide the music. A *Duffy's Tavern* sketch, minus Duffy and Ed Gardner, is performed by Eddie and Charles Cantor. Here is an excerpt:

HOPE making the announcements: Thank you, Paul Whiteman. This afternoon on your radio *Hall of Fame*, you and Philco, in honoring *Duffy's Tavern* program, have installed two characters in this season's show in the *Hall of Fame's* chamber of popular radio programs. The first is Clifton Finnegan, portrayed by radio's most versatile actor, Charlie Cantor, who in fifteen years of network performance has played everything from comedy to serious drama. Fred Allen fans will remember him fondly as Mr. Nussbaum and Socrates Mulligan, characters he has enacted on Fred's show for ten years. The other *Duffy's Tavern* standby is Archie's Jack of all Trades, and Master of Fun, Eddie the waiter, in the person of Eddie Green. Eddie has starred in those Negro classic comedy sketches called Heroes Are People on the old *Maxwell House Showboat*, and was featured in the Broadway hit the *Hot Mikado*, has been in numerous other stage shows and motion pictures. So let's accentuate the positive, eliminate the negative and don't mess with Mr. Eddie Green, at least not with his introduction, instead, let's have the man himself, and of course, Finnegan:

HOPE: Well, well, Eddie the waiter and Clifton Finnegan. Welcome to the *Hall of Fame*. It's good to see you both again. I remember the last time I ate at *Duffy's Tavern*, Eddie, I think you waited on me.

EDDIE: That's right, Mr. Hope. It is an old custom whereby the party of the first part leaves a tip for the party of second part.

HOPE: I left a tip, you should have looked under the plate.

EDDIE: I did and all I found under that plate was "made in China."

HOPE: Well, my autograph was right next to it.

(Slight break in conversation.)

EDDIE: Yeah, well, you see, right after the Academy Award dinner we expect to get a big crowd down at our place, and Archie would like to hire you as an entertainer.

HOPE: Oh no, I'll probably be busy that night, there's a rumor started that I'll win the Academy Award.

EDDIE: How you know?

HOPE: I started it. (Hope laughs.) Eddie, why wouldn't I win the Academy Award, after all, six million people saw me in my last picture.

EDDIE: Mr. Hope, six million soldiers eat beef on a shingle and it still ain't popular. (Soldiers in the audience begin whistling and clapping.)

On January 5, 1945, the *Duffy's Tavern* episode features Archie considering quitting, and he has a heated conversation with Duffy, that ends with Archie saying, "Aw go soak your feet, you big mullet head!"

EDDIE: Aw me, such a tender parting.

ARCHIE: Well, it's no use leavin' bad friends. Well, Eddie, I guess I'd better pack me stuff. Now, let's see here, where's me bartender's handbook?

EDDIE: You mean, how to win friends and put people under the influence?

ARCHIE: Yea.

During this program, Eddie sings "Candy," a popular song with music written by Alex Kramer, and lyrics by Mack David and Joan Whitney, and which was published in 1944. This song was recorded by various artists including, Big Maybelle, Dinah Shore, and years later, The Manhattan Transfer.

Jubilee, once again, presented another fantastic program on February 20, 1945. Billy Eckstine and His Orchestra start the program off with "Opus X." Eddie and Ernie Whitman perform a comic routine, and then they sing Hy Zaret's "One Meatball."

Hy Zaret was an Academy Award-nominated songwriter and lyricist, born August 21, 1907, in New York City. He wrote "One Meatball" with Lou Singer in 1924. "One Meatball" was also recorded by Tony Pastor, The Andrew Sisters, and Frank Sinatra with Lou Costello.

Mr. Zaret wrote lyrics for many songs and advertising jingles. His biggest hit was "Unchained Melody," with music by Alex North. It was written in 1955 for a movie called *Unchained*. Mr. Zaret and Mr. North were nominated for an Academy Award for best song. (Years later in July 1965, "Unchained Melody" again became a hit as sung by The Righteous Brothers.)

Hy Zaret was presented with numerous honors and awards for his works, including a George Foster Peabody Award, and the Ohio State University Institute for Education Award (twice). Hy Zaret lived a good long life, dying on July 2, 2007, at the age of ninety-nine.

By summer 1945, Eddie had begun courting my mother, and appearing on various programs around town, one of which was an AFRS program with Count Basie Orchestra and Hattie McDaniel. Eddie and Hattie had the audience laughing out loud with their skit, "Napoleon and Josephine." Following is a brief example. Ernest Whitman introduces Eddie Green and the Academy Award Winner Miss Hattie McDaniel. Ernest tells Hattie that Eddie is going to be Napoleon to her Josephine.

HATTIE: You mean I'm supposed to be in love with this little half-pint? My Goodness, K-ration love.

NAPOLEON (riding up on his horse): I hope Josephine is home, I got to get some money out of her, so I can get out of town.

(Napoleon gets to Josephine's, and goes in to greet her.)

JOSEPHINE: How come you love me so?

NAPOLEON: Josephine, let's not speak about money.

JOSEPHINE: We're not talking about money.

NAPOLEON: That's right, why don't we?

Now, by this time Eddie had become a superstar, thanks to the *Duffy's Tavern* radio program, and to performing in numerous other venues. I have made this determination because of the announcements that were beginning to appear in the local newspapers, such as:

"Coming May 1st. Orpheum – You've Screamed at Him on Duffy's Tavern – In Person – EDDIE GREEN."

Eddie was set to appear at the Orpheum in Los Angeles in a show that was headlined by The King Cole Trio and Johnny Otis and His Orchestra. Maybe they were referring to the audience screaming with laughter, but I like to think of people screaming and fainting, as if Eddie was a superstar.

The Duffy's Tavern radio program was well-received by audiences for its humor and for the guest appearances. The program was also recognized as being a leader in race relations. In Martin Grams, Jr.'s book, Duffy's Tavern, A History of Ed Gardner's Radio Program, Mr. Grams noted that "In early September, Duffy's Tavern received an honor unique in the entertainment industry." The radio program had been named to the Honor Roll of Race Relations by the Schomburg Collection of Negro Literature, for distinguished effort for improving race relations.

Similarly, in the Variety "1945 Show Management Reviews," it was announced that Variety had awarded a citation to Ed "Archie" Gardner's Duffy's Tavern, program, and the Danny Kaye show, for joint contributions towards improving race relationships. The citation read: In Abe Burrows' writing treatment of Eddie Duffy's Tavern Green, the Negro waiter, there's no attempt to build laughs perpetuating the weaknesses that have been the stock-in-trade of all Negro characters. Green clicks as a waiter, not because he's a Negro, but because he's good.

The movie, Ed Gardner's Duffy's Tavern, was an all-star musical comedy directed by Hal Walker. Along with Ed Gardner (Archie), Eddie Green (Eddie, the waiter), and Charles Cantor (Finnegan) playing the roles they normally played on the radio program. Paramount used a number of its great stars in the movie, all playing themselves: Bing Crosby, Betty Hutton, Paulette Goddard, Alan Ladd, Dorothy Lamour, Eddie Bracken, Brian Donlevy, Sonny Tufts, Veronica Lake, Arturo de Cordova, Phillip Crosby, Gary Crosby, Diana Lynn, Cass Daley, William Bendix, Maurice Rocco, James Brown, Joan Caulfield, Dennis Crosby, Lindsay Crosby, Gail Russell, Helen Walker, and Jean Heather. Also included in the movie were Barry Fitzgerald as Bing Crosby's father, Victor Moore as Michael O'Malley, Marjorie Reynolds as Peggy O'Malley, Barry Sullivan as Dan Murphy, Howard De Silva as the heavy, and Ann Thomas as Miss Duffy.

Reviews of the movie were mixed. The *New York Sun* reported: "Paramount has splashed all its marquee names into a Vaudeville show now running on the Paramount's screen as *Duffy's Tavern*. *Duffy's Tavern* is a jumble, sometimes funny, more often dull." This from the *Ballston Spa Journal*: "The *Duffy's Tavern* movie began a run at the Capitol Theater, the movie was "reputedly" an "entertaining bit of cinema."

The following telegram was received by and printed in the *Brooklyn Eagle* on September 6, 1945: "With 7,950 admissions at 1 o'clock, *Duffy's Tavern* opened yesterday to the biggest business of 1945 at the New York Paramount topping the year's record holder, Salty O'Rourke, by 650. Jack McInerney, N. Y. Paramount."

The article went on to say, "Ed Gardner is definitely IN! The famous radio comic turns out to be an ace comedian on the screen, in *Duffy's Tavern*, the new Paramount film at the N. Y. Paramount. It is based, of course, on the radio show of that name and Ed Gardner plays "Archie," the radio character he created. Everybody will be going to see *Duffy's Tavern* (observe the telegram above), but leave us hope that won't result in another epidemic of writers who inject leave us this and leave us that into every other line as their sole contribution to humor. It's catching. We're the first to admit it."

The movie made it to television a few years later. When I was about eight years old, my mom called me to the living room one evening and told me that I could stay up late that night and watch my father on TV. The night I saw him wiping down the bar at *Duffy's Tavern* was how I remembered him until I grew up. Prior to seeing Eddie on television, all I had was a vague memory of sitting on his lap when I was two or three years old.

After I saw my father in that movie, Eddie was always a "movie star" in my eyes; he was bigger than life. Unfortunately, I also resented him for dying before I could grow up.

Chapter Nineteen
Enter Norma Anne Murdock Amato, My Mom

My mom, at age twenty-two, was more than ready to leave her mother's house, and, besides, Eddie had a refrigerator. Not an "ice-box" but a real refrigerator. No more having to procure ice for the "ice-box." Whether she was in love with Eddie was never discussed with me, but I know in her later years, when speaking of him, she had a note of admiration in her voice. She appreciated the fact that he was a well-read, soft-spoken man, who was constantly working to better his knowledge. She liked to remind me of the fact that he spent most of his time at home tinkering with his ham radio and contacting people in all parts of the world.

The home that Eddie and mom moved into still stood as of 2016. Our house was located in Los Angeles, California in what is now known as the West Adams Historical District. Eddie was one of the first Black men to own a home in that part of Los Angeles, along with people like his buddy, Eddie "Rochester" Anderson. The property had a medium-sized front lawn and a large backyard, which is where my swing set was located. My swing set had a wooden seat. I still remember the time I got hit in the mouth by that seat, because I didn't get out of the way fast enough. I have a vague memory of the inside of the house. The walls were decorated with plates all the way around.

My bedroom was at the rear of the house with a window facing the backyard. We had a front "parlor" type room, which is where I practiced my tap dancing lessons. My memories of Eddie in that house are vague. He spent a lot of time away from home, while mom spent a lot of her time partying, which usually meant that I would wind up at my "Nana's" house, down the block. Our house became the "hanging out place" for Norma and her friends, especially as Eddie kept cases of liquor in the basement. Many a night, he would return home to no dinner because mom's day had been spent making Manhattans with her guests.

My mother was born Norma Murdoch on November 17, 1923. Her parents were what some might call an upper middle class family. Not because they had money, but because her mother, whose name was Sinclaire, by passing herself off as something other than a Black person, presented herself as such. Theirs was a household of untruths, confusion, and mental abuse. Sinclaire was not a particularly nice person, and would punish mom by taking her to the Orphan's Home on Adam's Boulevard and sit out front and tell mom that if she wasn't a better child, she would be returned to the orphanage. This caused my mom years of confusion as to her heritage.

Sinclaire, my grandmother, was born St. Claire White, in Chicago to Cora and Franklyn Pierce White, of Virginia. The couple migrated from Virginia to Chicago, where Sinclaire was born in 1896. She attended the Chicago Musical College, graduating in 1912 as the recipient of the Diamond Medal Award in the Teacher's Certificate Class. As a violinist, she played the first and second movements of Sitt's concertina in A minor, at her commencement. After graduation, she and her mother Cora, were to leave for Russia, where Sinclaire was to study violin for the next five years, according to an article in a 1912 issue of *The Crisis* magazine, which was published by W. E. B. Dubois, vol. 4 number 4.

I don't know if Sinclaire made it to Russia, and subsequent information I discovered during my research, which I will touch on further in this book, seems to suggest that she did not get to Russia. When I began writing this book, I could find no mention of Sinclaire again, until I located her in California eight years later. The 1920 census lists her as married to Alfonso Murdock and living in Pasadena.

My great-grandparents had also moved to Los Angeles, and in 1919 were living on East 45th Street, where Sinclaire and her husband were also living. At the time, she was giving violin lessons out of their home. I found an ad from a 1919 Pasadena newspaper announcing violin lessons, given by Sinclaire Murdock, B. A. with "Instruction in Scientific, Artistic Violin," on East 45th Street in Los Angeles. By 1930, the Murdock's had moved to Pasadena.

In 1929, Sinclaire was identifying herself as Spanish on my mother's school records, which contributed to my mom's befuddlement as to her own origins. Mr. Murdock, supposedly Sinclaire's husband and mom's father, was a Black man. Life for this family was going to change drastically within the next two years, but in the meantime, Sinclaire had begun holding weekly meetings of the *Sinclaire White Murdock Music Arts Association*, with her husband, Alphonso Murdoch, as Editorial Contributor. The meetings would proceed with musical selections and a reading of stories such as, "*The Immortal Story of Enoch Ardin*," by Sir Alfred Lord Tennyson. Sometimes, the meetings were held in the Second Baptist Church; other times meetings were held at the Sojourner Truth Home in Los Angeles.

After a *Music Arts Association* musical concert at the Second Baptist Church to "honor their sponsor, Mme. Sinclaire White-Murdock," where Sinclaire "graciously played two violin selections, "Variations" by Cesar Franck and "The Last Rose of Summer," a melody from the opera, *Martha,"* Sinclaire received a telegram of congratulations from Mr. and Mrs. Clarence Muse, according to the *Los Angeles California Eagle,* November 6, 1931.

To give you an idea of Sinclaire's talent, and because I absolutely love the wording of this article, I will print part of a rather lengthy column by Louis Michel from the *California Eagle* regarding the above concert:

"The violin deliverance of Madame Sinclaire White Murdock as epitomized in variations on DeBeriot's Air No. 11 and transcribed by Cesar

Franck on the violin, was a fountain of richest artistic beauty, a composite of lovely heights, depths and melodious elaborations of a violinist's greatest skill, such as only this divine artist can evolve. No one but she can transform this very heavy, and yet so charming work into the soul-depth and the sweetest interpretation that seemed to bewitch the audience of 700 people to such an ecstatic feeling that the entire flock of captive listeners was unable to master their unbridled amazement over the magical artist's unusually original playing. Truly, this was not merely Murdock, the fine pedagogue, nor Murdock, the leader of the *Music Art Club* that held forth, nor Murdock the noble, social entertainer and cosmopolitan mixer that was playing as was rarely heard in this city, but it was a Murdock entirely removed from her daily and weekly field of arduous teaching and organizing and lecturing. It was the divine Murdock that had left the entire arena of daily struggle and had flown to the highest spheres of God-inspired violin-virtuosity where only the genuine soul and her truest artistry had this woman so musically transformed into a different human being that dreamed more than she lived and that seemed embraced by loving Goddesses that took her away from this vulgar earth and gave her this most exquisite violin capacity to soar upward and heavenward . . . ."

This was the social Sinclaire at her best. As a wife and mother, she was someone quite different. She was an unfaithful wife. Sometimes she would take mom with her on assignations and leave her in, say, the "parlor" of a hotel room, while she went into another room with her "friend." Sinclaire had also been stepping away to Riverside, to visit her lover, Guiseppe "Joe" Amato, who had followed her from Chicago. Mr. Amato was an Italian man, who had been born in New York in 1896, after his parents emigrated from Italy.

One day, Mr. Murdock followed Sinclaire and found her with Joe. Murdock filed for divorce. During the divorce proceedings, Sinclaire revealed to him that, as a matter of fact, their daughter, Norma, was not his daughter, that Joe Amato was Norma's father, and that she, Sinclaire, also had a son by Mr. Amato. The divorce was granted in May 1933. Mr. Amato was also married, and when his wife discovered his affair with Sinclaire, he also received divorce papers in 1933.

Now, here is an interesting fact that I discovered while researching genealogy sites: a 1913 marriage announcement of Sinclaire White (who was seventeen at the time), to a Mr. Guiseppe "Joe" Amato. I don't think Sinclaire went to Russia. I think she got pregnant with a son in Chicago, married Joe, got divorced, after which she married Murdoch. After her divorce from Murdock, Sinclaire married Joe, again.

My mother died before I discovered this information, though a couple of years before she passed, she did tell me that she suspected Joe Amato was her biological father. My mom looked like she was a White woman, with wavy auburn hair that reached past her buttocks. She was constantly being questioned as to her ethnicity. Early on, she lost a job with the telephone company because someone found out she identified as Black. As the years went by and because of her uncertainty, she began to tell people that she was a "gypsy," and she continued to do this throughout her entire life.

After Sinclaire's divorce from Murdock in 1933, and her subsequent marriage to Amato, the Amato family moved to Alhambra. Grandfather Franklyn and Grandmother Cora moved to the Westside in Los Angeles. Sometime between 1933 and 1940, Joe moved out and set up a barbershop business somewhere in Los Angeles. Grandfather Franklyn passed away, and Grandmother Cora followed him about three years later.

In 2015, five years after my mom died, I found the following article.

Norma Anne Amato,
"To My Dear Daddy."

Mom never mentioned this, but it does seem to corroborate the fact that Joe and Sinclaire were mom's true parents. The headline of this article was, "Student Day at Hamilton," and read thus: "The youth of Hamilton Church 18th and Naomi Avenue, of which Rev. S. M. Beane is pastor, will observe Methodist Student Day. An assistant highway surveying engineer in the business world, Norma Amato, who sings fluently in Italian, French and Spanish, will render a selection. Norma Anne Amato, 18 years old, daughter of Mr. and Mrs. Guiseppe (Joseph) Amato, who majored in music and graduated from St. Cecilia and Romona Convents, was the young lyric soprano soloist featured by the Daughters of the American Revolution at their National Convention banquet in Los Angeles."

This article reflects the fact that there was some positive action Sinclaire pursued with my mother. Mom learned at a very young age to play the violin and the piano. Sinclaire also enrolled her in the Ramona Convent Secondary School, a Junior and High School in the San Gabriel Valley, in California. The school was, and is, "committed to providing a welcoming and inclusive Catholic environment in which young women integrate academic excellence, spiritual depth, personal integrity, and leadership skills as they prepare to meet the challenges of a global society." Norma became fluent in Latin, and was often asked to tutor other students in Mathematics.

My mother had aspirations to be an opera star and Sinclaire saw to it that mom had the best coach, Mme. C. Cahier, the former coach of Marion Anderson, one of the most celebrated Black opera singers of the twentieth century. Norma began performing for audiences when she was seven, usually at the Second Baptist Church, or at the *Murdock Music Arts Association*, and by 1942, she was singing at weddings, one being for the daughter of Rev. George Garner, of the Garner Music Center in Pasadena, and at social events at the *Wilfandel Club* in the Historic Adams District in Los Angeles.

In 1942, Mr. John Fowler, of the *California Eagle*, was quite impressed after hearing my mother perform on the piano and violin, printing in his column "Spreading Joy," "The stellar performer was Miss Norma Anne Amato, daughter of the famous concert artist, Mme. Sinclaire White Amato. Miss Amato first rendered 'Annie Laurie' in the transcription written exclusively for the left hand upon the piano, after which she played 'Souvenir' by Drdla, upon the violin. If Miss Amato was a grand pianist she was a grander violinist."

Norma had begun to get noticed for her talents, and, in 1944, had become Hattie McDaniel's protégé, which led to articles like this one in the *California Eagle:* "Miss Amato is the Talented Protégé of Miss McDaniel, representing Miss McDaniel as guest of Miss Lena Horne at her "after theatre" party closing her headline Orpheum appearance. Miss Norma, protégé of Miss McDaniel of *Gone with the Wind* fame, now seriously engaged in the study of voice, being also both Violinist and Pianist under her mother's tutorage. At present studying voice with the celebrated Mme. C. Cahier of Manhattan who is the former tutor and coach of Miss Marion Anderson."

The California Eagle printed a glowing account of my mom, prior to a performance at the Garner Music Center saying, "The beautiful and talented protégé of Miss Hattie McDaniel, the first Negro actress to win an Academy Award, will sing at Garner Music Center tonight. Her name is Norma Amato, and she has a voice as lovely as a tune by Jerome Kern." And I found this little blurb in another article, "Tip to Talent Scouts: Keep your ears on Norma Amato's delightful thrushing. She has the kind of voice you hear only in a dream."

Norma was also a social favorite when it came to hosting important events in the now Historic Adams District of Los Angeles. When Dr. Alain Leroy Locke, Howard Faculty Member, visited Los Angeles, Dr. Locke was the guest of honor at a dinner party and reception hosted by Dr. Isadora Mitchell. The majority of guests who attended the affair in honor of Dr. Locke were graduates of Howard University. Acting as hostess for the occasion was Miss Norma Amato.

On November 17, 1944, Norma Murdock Amato became twenty-one years old. At the time, she was still living with her mother, Sinclaire, and itching to get out. One year later, mom had finally left her mother's home and was married to Eddie.

Chapter Twenty

Living the Good Life

E ddie and Norma either were very quiet about their courtship or simply were not seen together often, so when Eddie and Norma eloped, it was a complete surprise to even their closest friends. They were married on October 30, 1945, in Yuma, Arizona. Once again, Eddie was in the headlines. "Eddie Green Takes Bride," proclaimed the *Pittsburgh Courier*. Mom and Eddie stayed a few days in Arizona before heading home.

November 9, 1945, *Duffy's Tavern,* now in its sixth season, aired an episode titled "Eddie Quits." Archie has just gotten off the phone with Duffy:

ARCHIE: Eddie, you're not serious, where did you get this idea about leaving?

EDDIE: Just looked into my wallet, and there it was.

ARCHIE: This is madness, you can't leave here, why, you're a part of Duffy's Tavern.

EDDIE: Yea, the part that goes over the cash register last.

ARCHIE: Just a second now, Eddie, is it that you're feeling that Duffy ain't done right by you?

EDDIE: Well now, you know yourself, when it comes to blowing that horn of plenty, he ain't no Harry James.

ARCHIE: Eddie, leave us discuss this, I think if you're fair minded I can show you that you're making a mistake. Now answer me this, do you object to working seven days a week?

EDDIE: Definitely.

ARCHIE: I suppose you object to putting in fifteen hours a day.

EDDIE: Very definitely.

ARCHIE: I suppose you also object to not being paid no salary.

EDDIE: Extremely definitely.

ARCHIE: Eddie, I'm afraid you didn't enter this discussion with an open mind. Don't you realize there's more important things than money?

EDDIE: Yea, but they all cost money! Look Mr. Archie, now, I'd like to have a salary, I just can't get along with the tips I collect.

ARCHIE: Aw now, don't hand me that Eddie. I've seen nights when you walked out of here with enough quarters to choke a horse.

EDDIE: Or kill him with lead poison. Mr. Archie, I just can't do it, in addition to the tips, I think I ought to have a dollar a week salary.

ARCHIE: How does 35 cents hit you?

EDDIE: It don't even muss my hauh.

Eddie and Norma started 1946 off with a bang, by hosting an Old Pals Club New Year Festival. The Old Pals Club was a social club made up of men and women who, as children, had played together and attended the same schools. The club met on a regular basis in various homes and periodically held holiday gatherings. As Eddie and Norma both were now well-known, this affair made the papers, namely, the *Los Angeles California Eagle*, which is where their social life usually played out. They set up a bar in the house, calling it Duffy's Tavern, where drinks were served and guests ate "traditional" New Year's Eve dishes such as hog maws and black-eyed peas. Their guest list included some of the luminaries and celebrities of the day, such as Hattie McDaniel, Mr. and Mrs. Mantan Moreland, Clarence Muse, Louise Beavers, Leon Washington, Jr., Vivian Dandridge (sister of Dorothy,) Rev. and Mrs. George R. Garner, and Mr. and Mrs. Ernest Whitman.

According to my mother, Eddie loved to have friends at the house, and there usually was a lively bunch hanging around. Mom put her opera studies on hold and began to practice being the "hostess with the mostest," as she herself used to say. When she and Eddie were not traveling, there always seemed to be banquets, benefits, weddings, baby showers, and luncheons to

Norma Green, Eddie Green, Louise Beavers, William Beavers (father of Louise Beavers), Hattie McDaniel, and an unknown guest. Photo courtesy of the California African American Museum.

attend, and Eddie liked to make appearances at the clubs on Central Avenue, so they had an active social life.

February 12, 1946, the *Pittsburgh Courier's* First Annual Sports Award Banquet was held in the ballroom of the Elks Temple, BPOE No. 9, in Los Angeles. The purpose of the banquet was to "create and perpetuate a fund with which to aid Negro high school and college athletes who would like to further their educational and athletic careers, but who lack the necessary monies to do so." The program honored such athletes as Joe Louis, Claude (Buddy) Young. Kenny Washington, and Jackie Robinson. Eddie appeared along with Lena Horne and the King Cole Trio.

Two months later, The Greens gave a "fabulous soiree" to celebrate the fact that Eddie had purchased the first television in the neighborhood. Miss Jessie Mae Brown, Society Editor for the California Eagle, was among those invited, and she reported that due to the newness of television, she was certainly looking forward to the event. My mom liked to say that Eddie was ahead of his time. When he got the television set, he cut a hole in the wall that separated the kitchen from the living room, setting the television in the hole. Mom said the only problem was that when she went into the kitchen, all she could see was the back of this huge contraption sticking out into her kitchen.

In May, Eddie announced that he was in the process of writing new material for a series of twelve featurettes, which would go into production in September in a Hollywood studio, Bell International. He informed the media that his productions would be musical comedies and would feature suntanned dancing beauties. In the midst of this, Eddie performed at the Orpheum in Los Angeles on the same bill with the King Cole Trio.

Norma was also busy being out and about, continuing to garner attention. A *California Eagle* columnist "spied pretty Norma Green" on the town. Norma had her own circle of friends to keep her busy in Los Angeles. Among her closest friends was Dr. Arthur Mitchell, who would become quite instrumental in our lives. Dr. Mitchell was an up-and coming obstetrician at the time. There was also Athenaise (Puffy) Hill (nee Houston). Puffy was the very socially active wife of John Lamar Hill. John, Puffy, and Norma and whoever she was dating at the time would often go out on the town before mom married Eddie. John Lamar Hill would later become the owner of Angelus-Rosedale Cemetery, Mortuary and Crematorium. Mr. Hill was also the original owner of KJLH, the first Black radio station in Los Angeles, which he purchased and ran for nearly fifteen years until he sold it in 1979. John Lamar would remain a friend of the family until his death in 1998.

That summer of 1946, during the break from season six of *Duffy's Tavern*, Eddie and Norma took a brief motoring vacation, driving to New York, Philadelphia, Pittsburgh, Chicago, and Baltimore. While in Baltimore, they had a brief interview with the *AFRO* newspaper. The *AFRO* spoke of Eddie as one of the country's leading comedians and questioned him on his thoughts regarding colored entertainers in radio. Eddie said that he had little doubt that there would be more roles for Black entertainers in radio, although he thought it might still be some time away. Of course Eddie was always optimistic about the abilities of Blacks to progress in any endeavor, but he was also realistic about the effort required in 1946 by Blacks to obtain roles in radio.

My mom spoke a bit during this interview about her ambition to become an opera star. She also spoke about what was to me a startling bit of news. She said that she had recently turned down an offer of the major singing role in the stage play *Carmen Jones* to remain in Hollywood with her husband. This was news I had never heard. Mom was generally reluctant to discuss her early years with Eddie, but to my way of thinking this was big news. No, this was startling news. My mother turned down a sure chance at fame to support her husband. For her, it was the right decision.

Though Eddie was working on getting his new movie studio off the ground, there was always time for something new. In July, he was given a part on a new radio program titled, *The Fabulous Dr. Tweedy,* starring Frank Morgan. Thaddeus Q. Tweedy was a doctor of philosophy and Dean of Men at Potts College for Girls. Eddie appeared in the recurring part of "Willie Beezer," the Train Porter. Other principal actors in the cast included Gale Gordon and Harry Von Zell. The series ran from June 2, 1946 until March 3, 1947. Morgan became a Hollywood character actor, best known for his role as "The Wizard" in *The Wizard of Oz* (1939).

Chapter Twenty-One
Sepia Productions, Inc.

Upon returning to the West Coast, Eddie announced the opening of his new film company, Sepia Productions, Inc., with himself as President, Mr. Seymour Simmons as Business Manager, and Mr. Harry Levette, as Publicity Director. Eddie had spent many months looking into the workings of Hollywood and the field of distribution before starting up his company. His idea was that he would provide musicals which would be modern and true to life, with all-Black casts in roles that were minus the stereotypical casting of which he thought Blacks had begun to tire. He had scheduled shooting for the first of his endeavors to begin in late July, probably due to the fact that *Duffy's Tavern* would be on summer vacation. He found a studio, located on Western Avenue in Los Angeles, which also doubled as a television studio.

Eddie began work on his first Sepia Productions film titled *Mr. Atom's Bomb*. The film was scheduled for release in late November of 1946, with Louise Franklin, Kitty Billbrew, and the Stanislaus Brothers, from the Hidden Talent Club. Due to what I like to call "the vicissitudes of life," the movie would not be released until April 1949 with a somewhat different cast and a new name.

Louise Franklin was a talented star of the stage at the time, performing at venues such as the Club Alabam on bustling Central Avenue in Los Angeles. Before signing with Sepia Productions, Franklin appeared in the comedy, *Two in a Bed,* with veteran actress, Louise Beavers, and in *Lady Luck* (1942).

Eddie's publicity director, Harry Gustavus Levette, was a veteran of the stage, movie and newspaper businesses. Harry was born on November 28, 1883, in Bridgeport, Ohio. He worked as a manager for Vaudeville shows for the *Tivoli Theater* before becoming an actor in such movies as, *Four Shall Die* (1940), and *Lady Luck* (1942). Mr. Levette was also a nationally known, long-time sports and theatrical writer for the *Associated Negro Press,* and before becoming Publicity Director of Sepia Productions, he had been the theatrical editor for the *Los Angeles Sentinel* newspaper.

As organizer, President, and coach of the Hidden Talent Club, Mr. Levette was instrumental in providing a place for those interested in becoming part of the world of entertainment. The club became widely-known through performances given by its members at various events, such as its benefit for the Yellow Jacket Sightless Club, which featured ballad stylist Barbara Harris, tap and boogie dancer Clayborn Williams, and concert soprano Queenie Jackson. The Hidden Talent Club also provided a special program as memorial for J. B. Bass (husband of Charlotta) Lodge in Watts, California, featuring Queenie Jackson, pianist and actress Antoinette Gibson, Clayborn Williams, Barbara Harris, and Eddie (Jazz-bo) Williams.

Mr. Levette provided talent for Eddie's first Sepia Production movie, including the Stanislaus Brothers trio and Miss Kitty Billbrew, who was lucky enough to be sent oversees to perform with the USO in 1946, and who had also worked with the Jester Hairston's sextet, General White and the Ten Dancing Darlings. Mr. Levette passed away in October of 1961.

Seymour Simmons, born January 14, 1896, began his songwriting career in the early 1900s. He was a prolific composer, writing over 800 songs, including "All of Me" in collaboration with Gerald Marks. In the late 1930s, Mr. Simmons was a radio producer and conductor of the Seymour Simmons Dance Orchestra. He became ill in early 1949 and passed away on February 13, 1949.

By August 1946, Eddie had sent out a call for "ten chickadees" to put in a chorus line for his upcoming movie. He also placed a "Talent Wanted" ad in which he asked for singers, dancers, and comedians to contact or call his office at 2640 ½ South Western Avenue in Los Angeles, telephone number WAY-4436.

On August 16, 1946, Eddie's fifty-fifth birthday, he appeared again on the *Fabulous Dr. Tweedy* radio program. One week later, he made an appearance on the *Beulah Show* radio program, which, at that time, starred a White actor, Bob Corley, as Beulah. Hattie McDaniel, would take over the role of Beulah in November 1947, becoming the first black woman to be the star of a network radio program.

On October 18, 1946, *The Daily Argus*, of Mount Vernon, New York, featured Eddie in an ad as "Eddie, the Waiter," promoting the local Community Chest Red Feather services, an organization providing help for people in need. Eddie was quoted as saying, "Nice thing about your Community Chest is that it benefits everybody in town. When there's anybody in trouble, when anyone gets sick, your Community Chest Red Feather services . . . the clinics, hospitals, the child care and youth agencies . . . are right there on the job. That's why I'm glad to give." The Community Chest is now known as the United Way, though there are still charities that continue to use The Red Feather symbol, which stands for community involvement and donations to those in need.

On November 6, 1946, Eddie and mom gave a lavish party in their home on Second Avenue in Los Angeles to mark their first wedding anniversary. Guests included Hattie McDaniel, Louise Beavers, Ben Carter, Harold Nicholas, Fayard Nicholas, Nicodemus Stewart, Ernest Whitman, Rev. George Garner, and Dooley Wilson (aka "Sam", the piano player in the movie *Casablanca*). They were treated to a buffet and cocktails.

A few days later, Eddie was interviewed by the *Los Angeles California Eagle*. The piece begins: "Dear Readers: We want to introduce to you this week, Eddie Green, the ace comedian of the air waves, whose part in *Duffy's Tavern* has shown that it is entirely possible for a man to be integrated into any sort of program regardless of race or color." "It's grand," Eddie Green said, "working with this show. The informality of it, the tavern setting (with a bar, tables and all this tavern equipment), and the lines, which I never have to worry about, turns work into play."

There was mention of the fact that Eddie was an amateur radio hobbyist with the call letters W2AKM, and that he was thrilled to talk to people all over the world. Evidently, his food choices were relevant, and Eddie told the interviewer that he liked, "old-fashioned ham and cabbage," which Norma was "super at cooking."

Season seven of *Duffy's Tavern* had begun broadcasting from their studio in Hollywood, on October 2, 1946. *Duffy's Tavern* had now completed 214 episodes, performing two live broadcasts a night, one performance for the East Coast and a second for the West Coast, plus rehearsals, and the show was still going strong, with the season running through June 25, 1947.

On the December 18, 1946 *Duffy's Tavern* episode, actress Joan Bennett from the movie *Woman in the Window* appeared as that week's guest. The tavern was going to raffle off a diamond tiara. Here is a sample of dialogue between Archie and Eddie with an example of Archie's proclivity for malapropisms:

ARCHIE: What are you thinking of giving your girlfriend, Sonia Jones, for Christmas?

EDDIE: Well, according to my wallet, a matched set of excuses.

ARCHIE: Oh, no dough.

EDDIE: That's right, and with Sonia, no dough, no soap. Women, why do they have to be that way?

ARCHIE: Well, Eddie, it's been a problem since time was immoral, you know. Anthony had that problem with Cleopatra, Napoleon had it with Josephine.

EDDIE: You mean, Josephine was wallet-minded, too?

ARCHIE: You seen pictures of Napoleon with his hand inside his coat?

EDDIE: Yea.

ARCHIE: What do you think he was holding on to? But, she loved him, Eddie.

EDDIE: Yea, but the trouble is, Sonia never studied history. And Napoleon didn't have the competition I got.

ARCHIE: Competition?

EDDIE: She got one boyfriend that makes perfume, a jeweler, then there's another one. . . .

ARCHIE: Just a second, if she's got all them boyfriends, why do you bother to give her anything?

EDDIE: I'm number three on the list, and I don't wanna lose my rating.

ARCHIE: Why don't you buy one of these raffle tickets? If you win, you can give her the diamond tiara.

EDDIE: That phony hunk of ice?

ARCHIE: Does she have to know its phony?

EDDIE: I forgot to tell you, she got another boyfriend that's a glass cutter.

During season seven of *Duffy's Tavern*, Eddie had begun working with Mantan Moreland in the movie *Mantan Messes Up*, along with Monte Hawley and Lena Horne. While working on the movie, Eddie got an opportunity to work on the *Amos 'n' Andy* show. Eddie had done one or two *Amos 'n' Andy* shows in 1942 and 1943, but the new part for which he was hired to play, lawyer LaGuardia Stonewall Jackson, would have a greater presence and would have more permanence. Eddie, of course, seized the opportunity.

Amos 'n' Andy, was the first radio program to be distributed by syndication in the United States, originating from station WMAQ in Chicago in 1928. This 15-minute daily situation comedy became probably the most popular radio show of all time. The listening audience was estimated at 40 million, almost one-third of Americans living at that time. Over the years, *Amos 'n' Andy* would be sponsored by Pepsodent, Campbell Soups, Lever Brothers, Rexall and Rinso. It was written and voiced by white actors Freeman Gosden and Charles Correll, performing minstrel-style as Black characters, located first in Chicago and later in Harlem.

Gosden and Correll played Amos Jones and Andrew Hogg Brown, respectively. They owned the Fresh Air Taxi Company, so-called because its only cab had no windshield. Gosden also voiced the character of George (Kingfish) Stevens, the third buddy in their weekly antics. In the early years "Sapphire," Kingfish's wife, was voiced by a White man, but in 1939 Ernestine Wade took over the role of Sapphire Stevens.

Freeman F. Gosden was born in Richmond, Virginia in 1899. After his service in World War I, Freeman became a radio comedian. He teamed up with Charles Correll and eventually their collaboration led to the *Amos 'n' Andy* Show. Freeman Gosden died December 10, 1982, in Los Angeles, California.

Charles James Correll was born in Peoria, Illinois in 1890. Charles spent his early working years in various professions, even as a bricklayer, before teaming up with Gosden. Charles Correll died September 26, 1972, in Chicago, Illinois.

Ernestine Wade was born in Jackson, Mississippi, in August of 1906. Acting since the age of four, her biggest claim to fame was her role as Sapphire, a role that she continued to portray when the program moved to television in 1951. Miss Wade would pass away on April 15, 1983.

Amos and Andy were the commonest of common men, they were the symbol of the "poor Joe," a guy with no money, no job and no future. *Amos 'n' Andy* became such a popular radio program that at the peak of its popularity movie theaters would stop their programs for fifteen minutes to let the audience catch the program over the theater loudspeakers.

The theme song for *Amos 'n' Andy* was "The Perfect Song," written by Joseph Breil for the movie, *Birth of a Nation* (1915). That last little fact about the theme song gave me pause when I first read of it. I have known for years that the National Association for the Advancement of Colored People (NAACP), had protested the portrayal of Black stereotypes on the *Amos 'n' Andy* show, but I have supported those roles as a way for Black people to make a substantial amount of money, which, at the time was not the case in other job markets.

To some people, the use of the theme song from a blatantly racist movie seems like an insult to Black people acting in and watching the show. This caused me to wonder why Eddie would consider being a part of the program unless it was to further his career or allow him to make more money that he could then funnel into his new movie venture.

I have watched the movie and listened to the song. The song is beautiful. I discovered that "The Perfect Song" was used as a theme song for the principle love story of the movie. This is the song that is heard whenever the two lovers, Elsie and Ben, meet. It is possible that the *Amos 'n' Andy* radio program used the song because the shows two principal characters, Charles Correll and Freeman Gosden, worked well together and loved what they were doing. The song may also have been used because these two principal characters were White men pretending to be Black, which mirrors *Birth of a Nation*, a movie with a large cast of White men and women in blackface. The truth is that *Amos 'n' Andy* provided work for Black actors and helped further Eddie's career. Once the program switched over to television the theme song was changed to Gaetano Braga's "Angel's Serenade."

In 1943, the *Amos 'n' Andy* radio program switched from a 15-minute CBS weekday dramatic serial to an NBC half-hour weekly comedy. The new version was a full-fledged sitcom in the Hollywood sense, with a studio audience (for the first time in the show's history) and orchestra. More Black actors were brought in to fill out the cast. In 1946, Eddie's role was as the lawyer LaGuardia Stonewall Jackson. On September 20, 1947, the well-loved ex-Mayor of New York Fiorello LaGuardia died and the name was shortened, making Eddie's role that of "Stonewall" Jackson.

The *Amos 'n' Andy* radio show received much criticism from the NAACP and others for its portrayal of Blacks as lazy and shifty, or loud and obnoxious, and for their characters' use of malapropisms. In reality, misspeaking a funny incorrect word for a similarly-sounding correct word had been a staple of comics for years. The character of Archie in *Duffy's Tavern* was famous for his use of malapropisms, which Ed Gardner used successfully to get laughs.

When *Amos 'n' Andy* became a television program in 1951, the NAACP protesters became insistent that the show be cancelled. Some say that after WWII, Blacks were more sensitive to how they were perceived by White society, and therefore did not appreciate seeing crooked Black lawyers or dim-witted Black cab drivers on television. The television show was cancelled in 1953 due to the fallout from the protests, but re-runs were broadcast until 1966.

Before the 1960s, shows that provided work for Black actors on radio and television were few and far between. An actor must act, and they need to eat and pay their bills. If an actor hopes to get ahead, they accept parts and play those parts to the best of their ability, because it is what they love. Eddie loved what he did, and I have to say that some of the *Amos 'n' Andy* skits in which Eddie appeared are still laugh out loud funny.

In an episode from late 1946, Eddie appears as LaGuardia, not as a lawyer, but as Kingfish's friend, who agrees to drive Andy around while Andy is on his vacation. Kingfish, in a scheme to move into Andy's room while Andy went on vacation, has sold Andy a trailer. Unfortunately, the trailer breaks down, so Kingfish has to find someone to be Andy's chauffeur. In that scene, we hear the door to Andy's place open and close:

ANDY: What you want?

KINGFISH: Andy, I really got some good news for you, son, I got a man with a car that'll go fifty-fifty with you on taking a trip with your trailer. You remember the lawyer, LaGuardia Stonewall?

ANDY: Oh yeah, sure, I know him.

KINGFISH: Well, he just went down to the five-and-ten cent store to get himself a pair of glasses, and, you see, he don't believe in eye doctors. He said that he'll be over here in front of your office with his car at 3:00 p. m.

ANDY: It's exactly 3:00 p.m.

KINGFISH: There he is now.

(Loud crash.)

ANDY: It's a good thing that other car was there, he'd of gone right past the office.

KINGFISH: There he is getting out the car, look at him.

ANDY: Got on his glasses, too, look at them things, they look like the bottom of milk bottles.

KINGFISH: Upsydaisy, he tripped over that fire hydrant and fell down.

ANDY: And he's the man who is going to drive me?

KINGFISH: Wait a minute. Come in, come in.

LAGUARDIA: Let me brush myself off. When I stepped out of the car a small boy tripped me up. Excuse me, gentlemen, I was lookin' for my good friend, the Kingfish.

KINGFISH: This is me over here.

EDDIE: Oh, yeah. Pardon me Kingfish, it's my new driving glasses. I don't see a thing.

KINGFISH: How is it working?

EDDIE: Oh, I still got to get a few bugs out of it.

KINGFISH: LaGuardia, I want you to meet my friend and your future vacation mate, Andy Brown.

EDDIE: Mr. Brown, it's a great . . . .

KINGFISH: No, no, that's the coat tree! Brown's over here.

ANDY: Kingfish, do you really think this is the man to do the drivin?

EDDIE: How are you Mr. Brown, and where are you?

ANDY: Here I is, and how's you?

KINGFISH: Why don't you take off your glasses, LaGuardia?

EDDIE: No, the girl behind the counter told me to keep them on and get used to them. You know I'm gonna do all my drivin in these.

ANDY: You got a driver's license, ain't you?

EDDIE: Oh sure I have, here it is right here.

ANDY: It says on here, this license not valid unless driver is wearing binoculars.

KINGFISH: He got enough glass on his nose there to make a telescope. We ain't gotta worry about nothing.

ANDY: You know, Kingfish, maybe we'd be better off if we just stuck his head down on the dashboard and drive by the instruments.

KINGFISH: You feel safe about this trip, don't you, LaGuardia?

LAGUARDIA: Well, if you want to make it 100% safe, just let Mr. Brown drive and let me lay back in the seat.

ANDY: I got a safer idea than that. If I go anywhere with you, I'm gonna walk. The deal is off, LaGuardia.

LAGUARDIA: Well, all right, that suits me, so long, boys.

KINGFISH: Look, Andy, I tell you what I'll do, I'll lend you my car and when you leave town, I'll even take your room off your hands.

ANDY: Now you're talkin', it's a deal. What'll we do about LaGuardia here?

KINGFISH: Oh, don't worry about him, he'll come out of that clothes closet after a while.

January 2, 1947, the cast of *Duffy's Tavern* moved to New York for approximately one month, then returned to Hollywood by February 12, 1947, where they remained through the end of the season. My mother, who was now twenty-three, did not go to New York. Instead, Norma spent her time being seen around Los Angeles. The writers of the society columns were taking note and keeping their readers up-to-date on her life, as society columnists are wont to do. Here is a blurb from the *Los Angeles California Eagle,* March 6, 1947: "Chatted with pretty Norma Amato Green, lookin' prettier than ever with the happy anticipation of becoming a mommy."

Yes, Norma was pregnant.

Chapter Twenty-Two

As the Stork Flies

E ddie tried various schemes in order to bring in money. For instance, he placed an ad in the local men's magazine, promising to deliver certain items to the purchaser if that person would send in $1 to his office on Western Avenue in Los Angeles. Mom told me that for quite a while she arrived at the office in the morning to find a number of envelopes on the floor with dollar bills in them, where they had been pushed through the mail slot. Of course, Eddie neglected to send whatever it was he had promised.

Eddie's office was also his television studio. He got the bright idea to dress mom as a "fortune teller," complete with a dot in the middle of her forehead, and then would do a one-minute spot for their television viewers, focusing on the astrological sign for that day. Eddie was the forerunner of television "fortune tellers." Full of ideas, was this man.

On March 30, 1947, Eddie was asked to emcee the floor show for the 68th Anniversary of the *California Eagle,* which was held at Meadowbrook Gardens in Culver City, California. Paul R. Williams, Architect, was guest speaker.

That same month, the 1941 film *One Round Jones,* Eddie's fourth movie, could be found playing at two theaters in Pittsburgh. One of the theaters, Fans, (seating 1800, it began as the Knickerbocker, and has since been demolished), was showing *One Round Jones,* along with *Woman in the Window*

(1944) with Edward G. Robinson. The second theater was the Pearl Theater, which has also been demolished. The Pearl Theater ran *One Round Jones,* along with *Ration Blues* (1943), featuring Louis Jordan and his Band.

March 20, 1947, Eddie took on his role as lawyer LaGuardia Jackson in an *Amos 'n' Andy* program titled "The Alligator Bag." In this episode, Andy bought an Alligator bag as a present for a young lady to whom he was attracted, but he gave the bag to her mother, not knowing that the lady in question was married. After this information becomes known to him, Andy needs to figure out how to retrieve the bag. Andy and Amos visit their lawyer:

ANDY: If I can get the bag back, I'll sell it back to you for what I paid for it.

AMOS: Well, here's our lawyer LaGuardia's office, let's go in and see if he can tell us how to get the bag back. Well, hello there, LaGuardia. Oh, uh, you got somebody in the office.

LAGUARDIA: Uh, Just a minute, boys. You say you want the marriage annulled?

CLIENT: Yes, it was all a mistake, and it took me ten years to find out!

LAGUARDIA: You ain't got nothing to worry about, because you see, with me on the case, it'll be a cinch. I'll meet you in court tomorrow morning at 9:00 a. m.

CLIENT: Thank you very much, goodbye.

ANDY: Who was that?

LAGUARDIA: My wife.

Back at *Duffy's Tavern* in Hollywood, season seven was in full swing. On May 28, 1947, *Duffy's Tavern* presented "Miss Duffy's Coming-out Party" with guest Bert Gordon:

Archie and Eddie are discussing the arrangements and invitations for the coming event:

ARCHIE: Well, it ought to be the biggest coming out party of the season, Eddie. We have a very exclusive guest list.

EDDIE: Very exclusive.

ARCHIE: Oh yes, by the way, did the invitations get out?

EDDIE: Oh yes sir, a kid's standing on the corner handing them out right now.

Availability is a key word for people in the entertainment industry, and in Hollywood there was always a benefit or two where major celebrities would gather. On June 14, 1947, Eddie joined Hollywood's celebrities at the West View Hospital Benefit, where "Tinsel Town's Top Stars Aid Los Angeles Hospital Campaign." This was a star-spangled benefit for the West View Hospital given by the Building Association at the Shrine Auditorium in Los Angeles. Harpo Marx was instrumental in arranging the guest list. More than 5,000 persons attended, including The Nicholas Brothers, Joe Louis, Suzette Harbin, Toni Harper, Leonard Reed, Peg Leg Bates, Cab Calloway, George Burns, and Eddie Green.

Approximately one week later, on June 22, at 11:15 p.m., according to the *Pittsburgh Courier*, "Eddie Green, widely known in stage and screen became the 'Proud Daddy' of a six-pound, seven-ounce infant. Norma, the former Norma Amato, Los Angeles beauty, and the baby, Elva Diane, were both doing well in the California Hospital."

About two months after I was born, the *California Eagle* did a piece on Eddie in their "Trail Blazers" column. The article spoke of Eddie's twenty-three years in show business, fifteen years of before-the-mike experience, and thirty years of technical radio knowledge. It mentioned his beginnings with "Fats" Waller in the 1920s and his progress to *Duffy's Tavern*. It also spoke a little about his days as a "Boy Magician," and of how Eddie began to be booked on all types of radio shows. This article also mentioned the fact that Eddie was a 32nd degree Mason and that he had spent the last year working actively with the NAACP.

The article quoted Eddie in regard to other ambitious artists wanting to get into the field of radio, "Radio for Negroes is a very hard field to get into . . . very hard! But the returns are so great that it's worth the try." Commenting further, Eddie said he found one thing to be true, "Talent is appreciated . . . you get respect if you know your business."

On November 2, 1947, a momentous family occasion occurred: I was christened by New York Congressman Adam Clayton Powell, Jr., who was also an ordained minister, at the Independent Church in Los Angeles, California, with Attorney Walter L. Gordon, Jr. standing as my godfather and my mom's friend, Mrs. Kay Seeley, as my godmother.

Walter L. Gordon, Jr., my godfather, was, in his own words, my father's "bosom buddy." Walter, born on June 22, 1908, (the same day I was born thirty-nine years later), was a prominent African-American attorney, who began his practice in 1936 in Los Angeles in an office on Central Avenue, and who did not retire until he was ninety-four years old. One of his more famous clients was singer Billie Holiday. Eddie and Walter became very close during the late 1940s.

(For a few years, my mother kept in touch with Walter. However, during the 1970s, she decided to sever all connection with him due to a misunderstanding on her part, and consequently, I, too, lost contact with him. After my mom died, I made it my business to get in contact with Walter, who at the time was 101 years old. I was able to visit with him at his home, where I showed him some recent pictures of mom, and we spoke of his relationship with Eddie. Walter spoke about how Eddie had simply "burst" onto the Los Angeles scene, after which the two of them had become "bosom buddies." Walter remembered mom as she looked years earlier, and he remembered

NEWEST 'MEMBER' OF DUFFY'S TAVERN IS CHRISTENED ON PACIFIC COAST IN CEREMONY
The Chicago Defender (National edition) (1921-1967); Dec 6, 1947;
pg. 18

NEWEST 'MEMBER' OF DUFFY'S TAVERN IS CHRISTENED ON PACIFIC COAST IN CEREMONY ATTENDED BY STAGE STARS

A FAR CRY FROM "DUFFY'S TAVERN" is this scene at Independent Church of Christ, Los Angeles, where the baby of radio star Eddie Green was christened. Left to right are Mrs. Eddie Green, the mother; Atty. Walter Gordon, Mrs. Roy Seel- ing, godmother; Eddie, Mrs. William Dickerson (holding baby Eva Diane) and unidentified guest; Adam Clayton Powell, New York Congressman; Rev. Clayton Russell, pastor of the church; another unidentified guest, and Rev. George R. Garner.

The *Chicago Defender* newspaper photo of me at my 1947 christening with the caption, "Newest Member of Duffy's Tavern Christened."

me, but he did not remember that he was my godfather. That was the last time I saw Walter, who passed away two year later.)

In 2014, while perusing newspaper articles in the Chicago Defender, I made an unexpected find—a photo of my christening in 1947, with all the parties involved. The caption read in part "Newest Member of *Duffy's Tavern* is christened." In the photo are my mother, Norma, Attorney Walter Gordon, Jr., Mrs. Roy Seely, my godmother, Eddie, Mrs. William Dickerson, Rev. Adam Clayton Powell, Jr., Rev. Clayton Russell, pastor of the Independent Church of Christ in Los Angeles, and Rev. George R. Garner.

I later found a separate article in the Gertrude Gipson column of the *Los Angeles California Eagle*: "The little darling of Eddie and Norma Green was christened by Rev. Adam Powell at the Independent Church Sunday with Atty. Walter Gordon, Jr. as godfather and unfortunately I didn't get the godmother's name."

Though I was not able to use the picture to refresh my godfather's memory, I was thrilled to have discovered it, especially as Rev. Adam Clayton

Powell, Jr., is in the picture. Rev. Powell was a Baptist pastor and Congress-man. Reverend Powell was a preferred choice for officiating at christenings and weddings by many Black celebrities. As a Congressman, he represented Harlem, New York, from 1945-1971. He was the first Black person from New York to be elected to Congress.

Chapter Twenty-Three
Business as Usual

Octobeber 1, 1947, *Duffy's Tavern* was back for their eighth season. On the November 5, 1947 episode, Archie is giving himself a surprise Testimonial dinner, and he is anxious that everything is in order:

ARCHIE: Eddie, did you chill the champagne, yet?

EDDIE: Chill it? I ain't even finished makin' it yet.

In February 1948, the Club Congo in Los Angeles, put together a four-hour festival featuring stars of stage and screen, as a benefit to raise money to help send kids to summer camp. The show featured over fifty performers, with special guest appearances by Ella Fitzgerald, Eddie Heywood, Lorenzo Flornoy, Bill Robinson, Louis "Satchmo" Armstrong, and, "Eddie Green of *Duffy's Tavern.*"

The next month, a decision by the Academy of Motion Picture Arts and Sciences resulted in a major event that occurred on March 20, 1948: Mr. James Baskette received an Honorary Academy Award for his performance as "Uncle Remus" in Walt Disney's *Song of the South,* making him the very first Black male performer to receive an Oscar.

The presentation was held at the Shrine Auditorium in Los Angeles, California. Screen actress Ingrid Bergman presented Mr. Baskette with the award. He said that he was "elated over the fact that he had done something

151

that would go down in the history of cinema." Afterwards, Mr. and Mrs. Baskette were entertained at the home of a friend. Eddie and Norma were included as guests. Eddie and Mr. Baskette, you will remember, worked together in the 1929 Broadway play, *Hot Chocolates*, and Mr. Baskette had a starring role in Eddie's 1940 movie, *Comes Midnight*.

The fact that an honorary Academy Award had been bestowed on Mr. Baskette was news to me. My mother never mentioned being present at the after party, and I do not remember this fact being discussed, for instance, before or after Mr. Sidney Portier won the Academy Award for Best Actor in *Lilies of the Field* (1963). It seems that Mr. James Baskette is another famous actor who paved the way but has faded from the scene.

In May 1948, Ed Gardner began to focus on his production of a stage play of *Duffy's Tavern*. By the middle of June, the play was at the New York Strand Theater, with four shows a day and five shows on Saturday. Eddie was given the opportunity to showcase his talent with a solo "poker trick" pantomime that was very popular. Probably something learned during his early years as a magician. The play was well-received and was presented through June 23, 1948, which ended the season.

On June 26, 1948, a floorshow and dance was presented at the Bowman's Rainbow Restaurant and Eddie was the honored guest. The Debonairs performed their first floor show and dance that evening, with entertainment provided also by Al Hibbler, a baritone vocalist, who sang with Duke Ellington's orchestra before having several pop hits as a solo artist. Mantan Moreland was on hand, as well as Manhattan Paul, born Paul Bascomb, known for his stylings with the tenor sax and, who became a singer with the Manor and Atlantic record labels. In attendance also were dancer Bobby Lopez and Carl Van Moone, "vocal discovery of 1948."

This summer had its highs and lows. My maternal grandmother, Sinclaire White Amato died on June 29, 1948, at the age of fifty-two. I was never able to get my mother to discuss any details about the death or the whereabouts of Sinclaire's gravesite.

Over these last couple of years, Eddie had been busy trying to get his fifth movie off the ground. Maybe someone had knowledge of this fact— similar to what is done today—Eddie's fourth movie, *One Round Jones*, which premiered in 1941, was playing again at The Vogue Theater in Philadelphia, along with *Daisy Kenyon* (1947) starring Joan Crawford. For this movie to be playing seven years later, perhaps someone was anticipating Eddie's upcoming movie and was determined to profit from that event. The Vogue Theater, one of the only theaters that showed "Colored" movies at the time, was later turned into a church.

While researching The Vogue Theater, I discovered that the street name of the address had been changed from Columbia Avenue to Cecil B. Moore Avenue. Mr. Cecil Bassett Moore, born April 2, 1915, was a Black Philadelphia lawyer and civil rights activist, who was credited with restoring order after the racially-charged Columbia Avenue Riot in North Philadelphia in 1964.

Cecil B. Moore served nine years in the Marine Corps., sat on the Fifth District seat on the Philadelphia City Council, and served as President of the Philadelphia chapter of the NAACP. Mr. Moore died February 13, 1979.

One of the things that strongly interested Eddie was the field of television. In an interview with the *New York Age*, he said that "he believed the field of television was a fertile field for Negro performers, and for this reason his motion picture firm had already approached advertising agencies with ideas on how they can get sponsors to sell their products via the singing and dancing route." This is how Eddie proposed to aid show business through his television firm.

Eddie believed that Black performers should "demand that their agents establish connections with the television people so as not be left out in the cold." He thought the decline of Vaudeville left little hope for the birth of new talent, until television showed up with vast potentialities.

In August, Eddie added to his busy schedule and joined "Dizzy" Gillespie, the "King of bebop," The Four Step Brothers, tap dancer "Sandman" Sims, and many others, to perform at the Southeast Health Festival. The festival, the first of its kind, was organized and staged by the youth of the Southeast Youth Health Organization to allow them to show the Harlem community what they were doing to improve the community health.

That October, Eddie decided to branch out in a different direction in the moving picture business. According to the *Gloversville and Johnstown* New York newspaper, he took me in for a screen test at M-G-M when I was eighteen months old. (I learned about this during my research in 2014. I was floored when I discovered this information. I have no idea of the outcome of that screen test. Mom never mentioned it, which is probably best, as I have no desire to become a movie star, or as my mother would put it, "a moving star," although I can do a wonderful Gloria Swanson imitation!)

October 10, 1948, Eddie had a part in an *Amos 'n' Andy* sketch titled, "Lulu Mae Simpson Is Coming to Town." For your enjoyment, I am sharing a bit of the sketch that I found particularly funny. Stonewall shows up for an appointment with the boys:

KINGFISH: Well, Stonewall, the lawyer, come in.

STONEWALL: Yea, I'm sorry I was late, boys, I been in court today, defending a woman client.

KINGFISH: Oh yeah? What happened?

STONEWALL: Well, some woman called me up and asked me if I would defend her in court. You know, give her some tips on how to be.

ONE OF THE BOYS: Oh yeah, go ahead.

STONEWALL: I told her I couldn't get there until the last minute, but I would give her some advice on the phone and told her how to act goin' up to the witness stand. I told her, roll your eyes at the judge, smile and wink at the judge, wear a form-fitting satin dress with sheer nylon hose.

KINGFISH: How'd she come out?

STONEWALL: She lost the case. I didn't know she was ninety-six years old!

By now, some of Eddie's friends had begun to notice a change in his demeanor, and it was thought that he seemed a little under the weather. However, he was still accepting engagements like the one at Earl Carrol's famous Hollywood Restaurant. On November 4, 1948, a "mammoth" show was staged by the Benevolent Variety Artists. In attendance were stars such as Eddie "Rochester" Anderson, Toni Harper, Mabel Scott, Mantan Moreland, Howard Duff, Ed Gardner, Cab Calloway, and a host of other celebrities. During that month, Eddie also attended a benefit for the Sightless Club of America, with Ernest Whitman and Harry Levette. In December, Eddie made a one-time appearance on *Mirth and Melody*.

On December 26, 1948, *Amos 'n' Andy* broadcast an episode titled, "The Mysterious New Year's Card." George (Kingfish) receives a New Year's card from a woman, and in the process of trying to find out who sent the card, he winds up being sued by his wife for "separate maintenance." Here is an excerpt from the courtroom scene with Eddie playing "Stonewall" the lawyer:

ATTORNEY: Mrs. Stevens, do you think you could finish telling the court what happened?

MRS STEVENS: Well your honor, I was collecting for the welfare fund, and when I reached the top of the stairs by the door leading to Miss Jackson's apartment, the door opened and my husband come rushing out and almost knocked me down. He said, "Outa the way, madam, my wife is on her way up here." I seen it with my own eyes, and that's why I want separate maintenance.

JUDGE: That will be all. Does Mr. Stonewall, the attorney for the defendant, wish to cross-examine Mrs. Stevens?

STONEWALL: NO, man, I don't need to cross-examine her. She got the goods on him.

JUDGE: Order in the court. Continuing with the case of Stevens vs. Stevens. Attorney for the defense may now proceed.

STONEWALL: Your Honor, I would like to have my client, George Stevens, take the stand. Now Mr. Stevens, your wife stated you were absent from your home on various occasions. She further implied, that on these nights you were seeking feminine companionship with a beautiful girl. Was you? You rascal, you.

GEORGE: No, I was not!

STONEWALL: Well, nice going bub. Will you tell us in your own words what happened the night you lied to your wife about going to a lodge meeting, and went to see your sweetheart, Helen Jackson, instead?

GEORGE: Well, uh, uh I just went to see this Helen Jackson to find out if she sent me a New Year's card signed, your sweetheart. When she said she didn't, I rushed out of the apartment and I run into my wife just outside the apartment door.

STONEWALL: There your honor, that's my client's story. Which shows exactly what his intentions was. Never for one moment, was it in his plan to let his wife catch him in his girlfriend's apartment.

GEORGE: Now, wait a minute

STONEWALL: Don't worry, we got em rollin'. Your honor, I would like to review the facts at this point. The evidence against my client shows first, he stayed out late nights, second, he lied to his wife, and third, she caught him coming out of another woman's apartment. BUT NOW, let me list the overwhelming facts in FAVOR of my client. Now, one, Mr. Stevens never, er, uh, he wasn't the, uh . . . Your Honor, could we have a recess, so I can think of SOMETHING in favor of my client?

Listening to this skit causes me to laugh every time. I searched for and found this episode because I read a comment on the World Wide Web from a gentleman who thought this episode was one of the best and I thoroughly agree.

Just after Christmas, on December 29, 1948, *Duffy's Tavern* aired a program based on Archie, the manager, and the fact that he has a problem that he has not shared with Eddie or Miss Duffy. He is brooding in the backroom and is not available to answer the telephone when it rings, consequently, the telephone is answered by Eddie:

EDDIE: Hello, Duffy's Tavern, where the elite meet to eat, Eddie, the waiter speakin'. Oh, hello Mr. Duffy, I want to thank you for your Christmas present, a lovely cigarette lighter. Yeah, very thoughtful inscription, too: "Close cover before striking."

For a reason unknown to Miss Duffy and Eddie, Archie refuses to come out of the back room, and Miss Duffy is worried:

MISS DUFFY: Hey Eddie, is Archie still in the backroom? What's eating him?

EDDIE: In that back room, it could be anything!

To cap off 1948, Eddie and Norma threw a New Year's Eve party. There were celebrities and socialites at the Green residence that night, and of course, a member of the press was present to describe the gorgeous gowns worn by the women, and to record who was staring at whom. Those who stopped by included Mabel Scott, known for her songs, "Elevator Boogie" and "Boogie Woogie Santa Claus."

Chapter Twenty-Four

Mr. Adam's Bomb

On February 13, 1949, Mr. Seymour Simmons, the composer-conductor and business manager for Sepia Productions, Inc., died. I can only imagine the affect that may have had on Eddie, especially as he wasn't doing well himself. However, as they say, the show must go on, and on February 17, 1949, Eddie announced through the newspaper that he had begun rehearsals for his newest movie, *Mr. Atom's Bomb*, in his television studio. The movie was to be produced at Bell International Studio in Hollywood, California, and was to have an April premiere in New York City at The Apollo Theater.

Over time, the title of the movie was changed to *Mr. Adam's Bomb*, possibly because the former title was seen as being "politically incorrect," as we might say today. *Mr. Adam's Bomb* was produced, written, and directed by Eddie, who also starred in the movie, along with Mildred Boyd, Gene Ware, Leslie Mumphrey, and Jessica Grayson, and premiered at The Apollo Theater in New York the first week of April, 1949. It is unclear what happened with the 1946 plans for this movie. There are two existing posters for *Mr. Adam's Bomb*. One has a bright yellow background with the words Sepia Productions Presents Mr. Adam's Bomb in blue letters. Eddie's face is pictured in the center of the photo surrounded by the faces of five women whose names are unknown to me. On either side of Eddie are puffs of clouds that resemble atom bomb clouds. Since I do not know who the women are,

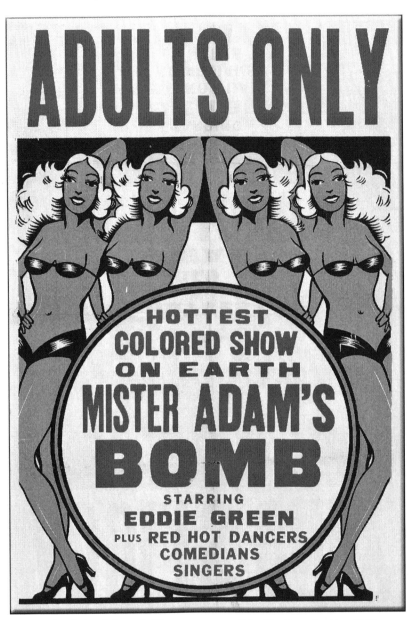

Mr. Adam's Bomb (1949). Photo courtesy of the Heritage Auction Gallery.

I have not included a picture of this poster, however, there is another poster for *Mr. Adam's Bomb* that declares in large letters "Adults Only," which I have included. Considering the fact that this poster features renderings of women clad in bikini bathing suits, it may be safe to assume this poster replaced the yellow poster for the purpose of diluting the atom bomb idea.

The storyline of *Mr. Adam's Bomb* involves members of a family who share a boarding house. The daughter of the family is having a coming-out party, and a number of guests have been invited. Unfortunately, Uncle Adam Jones, the upstairs boarder, has been acting rather secretive over the past few days, apparently trying to sneak packages up to his room.

The family members are still affected by the dropping of the Atom bomb in 1945, which causes them to be hypersensitive. They are afraid, even though they say that they know "Uncle Sam ain't gonna let nobody get the best of him." The family decides to hire a detective and have him come to the house under the guise of being a guest, so that he might be able to discover just what Mr. Jones is doing upstairs in his bedroom.

During the party, the guests are entertained, first with a magic act done by Mr. Jones and a guest from the audience (Eddie, the undercover detective,) while Eddie's partner searches Mr. Jones room. After the magic act, Miss Margaret Westfield performs a song written by Eddie, titled, "You Can Always Believe Your Heart," after which there is a dance performance by The Sepia Misses. The movie ends on a good note, when Mr. Jones gives his niece the coming-out present he had bought for her, which he had been trying to hide from prying eyes. Eddie shares a little homily as the film comes to an end with his face being the last thing you see in a little circle on the screen.

Eddie did not like sadness; he didn't even like to see comedians get booed off the stage. I imagine he chose to make this movie a musical as a way to provide some type of relief from the reality of the fear and suspicion that people were experiencing after the dropping of the atom bomb, the same way that Native American Indians tell the story of The Buffalo Dance, which helps them to come to grips with the necessity of killing buffalos. In any event, the movie went over well, prompting this statement from a Mr. Berman, manager of the Largo Theater in Watts, California, "I believe that my patrons would want to see this picture, not only because of the fact that it has an all-colored cast, but it features one of the best comedians in the country—Eddie Green."

The movie is catalogued in the Cumulative Catalogue of Motion Pictures, 1940-1949, as *Mr. Adam's Bomb*, Sepia Productions, Inc., with the summary being, "A comedy short about a young girl's coming out party."

Mildred Boyd, the daughter of the movie, was an actress and dancer, who had been in show business since the 1920s. She began with bit parts in silent films and went on to roles in Black Cinema, one of which was *Look Out Sister* (1947) with bandleader Louis Jordan. Miss Boyd also had a part as a maid in the Hollywood movie, *I Love a Bandleader* (1945) with Phil Harris and Eddie "Rochester" Anderson.

Gene Ware, the gentleman who played Adam Jones, was an actor, who, at one time, was "Pans" of "Pots, Pans and Skillets," and who was also slated to star in Nicodemus Stewart's musical, *This Is It*, along with Ernest Whitman and George Dewey Washington, before being cast in a principal role in *Mr. Adam's Bomb*.

Jessica Grayson was born on March 7, 1886. Miss Grayson was a veteran actress, who appeared in at least fourteen movies during her career, which included her role as, "Addie" in *The Little Foxes* (1941) with Bette Davis, as Violet in *Our Very Own* (1950) with Anne Blythe and Farley Granger, and as Ella Tearbone in *Syncopation* (1942) with Adolphe Menjou and Jackie Cooper. Miss Grayson died on February 27, 1953 in Los Angeles, California.

Leslie Mumphrey, was best known as one of the singing leads in Willie Covan's Glorious Bronze Review, *Up and At 'Em*. Willie Covan, a big-time tap dancer, had a dance studio in Los Angeles, California, in the mid-1930s.

A member of the fourth estate, as they were known in those days, printed an extremely complimentary article on April 12, 1949, after the release of *Mr. Adam's Bomb*." "One of Hollywood's producers, Eddie Green, recently produced, directed, and starred in an all-Negro film titled Mr. Adam's Bomb. Producer Green is probably better known to you as, Eddie, the waiter on "Duffy's Tavern." Also does Stonewall, the lawyer on Amos N Andy, started in show business as a magician, then went into Burlesque, where he worked with Abbott & Costello! And also did some musical comedies with Bill Robinson. Since joining Duffy's Tavern eight years ago he's never missed a program—no other member of the cast can make that statement."

On April 20, 1949, Cass Daley was the guest star on *Duffy's Tavern*. As well as performing in a skit with the crew, Miss Daley sang her version of Eddie's most famous song from 1917, "A Good Man Is Hard to Find." She had a loud singing voice, which was gravelly at times, so her version of the song was different than prior versions, very upbeat:

> "Now here's a story, with a morale,
> and all you gals better pay some mind,
> cause if you find a man worth keepin,
> be satisfied, be sure to treat him kind.
> Cause a good man is hard to find,
> you'll always get the other kind,
> just when you think that he's your pal,
> you turn around and find him messin' around some other gal.
>
> Then you rave, you even crave,
> you see him layin' right in his grave,
> so if your man is nice, take my advice,
> hug him in the morning, kiss him every night,
> give him plenty lovin, treat him right,
> because a good man nowadays is hard to find.
>
> Yes siree girls, you know,
> once I had a man of my own,

yeah, and since he's gone, boy,

I really miss him, you see,

most girls have to kiss a man to hold him,

but me, I have to hold 'em to kiss 'em.

He wasn't much good at culture

and he had a funny pan.

As a matter of fact, he wasn't much of anything,

but at least he was a man,

and if he comes back to my little grey shack,

I'm gonna hug him in the morning,

kiss him every night,

give him plenty lovin,

treat him right, because a good man, nowadays, is hard to find.

Yes siree folks, they say

that opportunity knocks but once,

and when that once is gone sister,

it's gone forever.

So girls, if you get a man

there's just one but,

keep a smile on your face,

and keep you big mouth shut.

I learned my lesson now and everything's fine,

and if he comes back I'll never, never step out of line,

cause I know what to do when the day is through,

gonna hug him in the morning,

kiss him every night,

give him plenty lovin,

treat him right, because a good man, nowadays, is hard to find."

The song was not prefaced with any type of introduction as to who the writer was, but maybe Eddie was so popular at the time that *Duffy's Tavern* fans knew he had written "A Good Man is Hard to Find" and therefore needed no reminder. Also, it is conceivable that the song was featured in that particular episode because Eddie's health could be seen by those who were working with him to be in decline.

In May, Eddie became quite ill. Those in the news industry who knew him decided that he was working too hard. It was said, jokingly, this might be a good thing, though. Pigmeat Markham and John Mason were quoted as saying, "Eddie has so much money now, that he has stopped counting it and started weighing it."

Eddie's declining health, and a need to take it easy, forced him to quit the *Amos 'n' Andy* show, though he was still busy looking for new talent interested in working in television. He had put together ideas for musical spots for advertisers that he was eager to put into action, and he was putting together plans for another movie.

June 29, 1949, season nine of *Duffy's Tavern* ended with episode #329. Ed Gardner made the decision to move his show, including his cast members and their families, to Puerto Rico, where they would begin season ten. On August 13, 1949, my mom, Eddie, and myself, left Los Angeles to live in Puerto Rico. Eddie was to work on his picture ideas while there.

Before Eddie left for Puerto Rico, he and my mom attended the Omega Smoker, a reception given in Mr. Paul R. Williams' house in Los Angeles for the Governor of the Virgin Islands. Among the guests present were Dr. Ralph Bunche, Jack Dempsey, and Roy Wilkins of the NAACP. Eddie took over the party by telling some of his "grandfather" jokes.

In the midst of getting settled in Puerto Rico, Eddie was asked to write an article for the 1949 September issue of *The Negro Digest*. The article, which follows, was titled, "My Biggest Break:"

"It was during the year 1929. I was living in New York and trying every kind of theatrical job that was available. I had already played all kinds of Vaudeville, Burlesque, musical comedy and a few small radio programs. I had tried everything except a colored Broadway show.

"In the meantime, I was so busy working here and there and doing a bit of writing on the side that I did not notice my own advancement. One indication of the change, I should have noticed, was the fact that I could see my name very frequently in the various trade papers. Then along came George Immerman and opened a show called, Hot Chocolates. I became the featured comic in this show. It turned out that none of the various scenes written for the show were good enough so I was engaged to write the scenes. With the material written by me, the show opened on Broadway and became one of the outstanding comedy shows of that year and ran for quite some time.

"During that time, Commander Richard E. Byrd decided to explore the South Pole. The National Broadcasting Company also decided to send some special programs made up of top-ranking radio people down there to entertain the Commander and his men. For one of these programs they selected, among the others, yours truly.

"The hitch was the program left here at 11:00 p.m. and I went on the stage for my last scene at that same time. The only way that I could appear on that program would be to find some way to get me out of the theater and down to the National Broadcasting Company immediately after the sketch. The Police Department solved the problem by giving me a motorcycle escort from the theater to the National Broadcasting Company studio.

To those who don't know, let me inform you that to rate a police escort in New York you must be somebody. It was during that wild ride, behind screaming police sirens up Broadway on the wrong side of the street with all of the theaters letting out, that I realized I had become "somebody." Yes, I began asking for more money."

Duffy's Tavern cast in Puerto Rico: Larry Rhine, Hazel Shermet, Ed Gardner, Charles Cantor, Eddie Green. Photo courtesy of Ed Gardner, Jr.]

Chapter Twenty-Five

The Ending

E ddie's health continued to decline in Puerto Rico. Soon after the beginning of season ten of *Duffy's Tavern*, he suffered a heart attack. Some
thought that it may have been the heat, or the fact that he worked too hard.
A rumor went out that he had died, but turned out that he was "ill, not dead."
Eddie told reporters that his schedule had "sapped some of his strength,"
which was why he had given up his role of "Stonewall Jackson" on *Amos 'n'
Andy*. In a photo at the bar in Puerto Rico, Eddie had begun to look very thin.

After a few weeks of recuperation, Eddie returned to his role on *Duffy's
Tavern* in December of 1949, under the care of his physician. Over the next
four months, Eddie continued to miss episodes due to his heart ailment, and
in May 1950, he retired from the world of show business.

On May 4, 1950, Eddie, my mom, and myself boarded the S.S. Puerto
Rico out of San Juan, and we arrived at the port of New York on May 8, 1950.
Eddie was taken to the Hotel Theresa, where he stayed for a short time be-
fore heading home to Los Angeles.

The Hotel Theresa, later known as Theresa Towers, was primarily an
apartment hotel, but they occasionally accepted temporary guests. The
hotel, which was built in 1912, was the tallest building in Harlem until the
Adam Clayton Powell, Jr. State Office Building was constructed in 1973.
Initially, the hotel was "Whites only," but in 1937, the hotel was bought by

Black businessman Mr. Love B. Woods, who effectively ended its segregation policy. While at the hotel, Eddie got it into his head to go to a nightclub, and wound up being escorted by a friend, back to The Hotel Theresa.

Articles appeared in various newspapers regarding Eddie's return and illness. The *Pittsburgh Courier* wrote, "Comedian Eddie Green's heart ailment has forced him to retire from show business. His retirement will sadden the hearts of all lovers of good entertainment."

Dorothy Killgallen, from the *Schenectady Gazette*, in her "Voice of Broadway" column, wrote, "Eddie Green, Ed Gardner's long-time aide on *Duffy's Tavern*, has quit the show, and is heading back to the US from Puerto Rico."

There was one particular comment in the *Long Island Star-Journal* that touched me. It read, "Eddie Green, suffering from a heart ailment, probably will be replaced permanently on *Duffy's Tavern*. Too bad." This comment showed me that there were people who were genuinely sorry about Eddie's circumstances, and were sad to see him leave the radio program.

By June, Eddie and mom were back at home in Los Angeles. At the beginning of June, Eddie was admitted into the Hospital of the Good Samaritan. By July, he was at home receiving visits from his physician. There were twelve home visits in July, and nineteen home visits in August. By the beginning of September, he had gone into a coma. My mom told me that before he lapsed into the coma, he had lost the ability to recognize her. His first-born daughter, Hilda, had arrived from Philadelphia to be by his side.

On September 5, 1950, Eddie was admitted to the Good Samaritan Hospital for the last time. He remained in the hospital receiving lab work and various drugs. On September 19, 1950, approximately one month past his fifty-ninth birthday, Eddie died.

News about Eddie's death and funeral was noted in various newspapers. The *Baltimore Afro American* printed an article that included a picture of Eddie and his boss, Ed Gardner. In the article, it was noted that Eddie had been given High Masonic Rites at his funeral, which was held at the Neighborhood Community Church, with Rev. H. Mansfield Collins delivering the sermon. The article made note of the fact that Eddie had been a member of the Shriners in Los Angeles and the Knights Templars in Buffalo, New York.

The *Pittsburgh Courier's* Billy Rowe gave the most moving tribute to Eddie in his article printed on September 30, 1950. Mr. Rowe talked about the people who were standing around Eddie's bed offering words of encouragement while Eddie was still in The Theresa Hotel after returning from Puerto Rico. He said, "Their words were shallow and their emotions were deep because within their hearts, they knew that the funny man was running this way for the last time. Just a few days ago Eddie departed this life and his death added to the sadness of the world."

The write-up from the *California Eagle*: "Eddie Green Is Buried in L. A. The beloved star of *Duffy's Tavern*, who captivated radio audiences for nine years, took his final call last Tuesday after a heart attack."

The Rev. H. Mansfield Collins was quoted as saying, "Eddie Green has pushed the shadows away and brought sunshine into the lives of many. Yes, Eddie played his part well on the stage of time."

It was noted that Hattie McDaniel was there "with tears streaming down her cheeks," and that, "Andy Razaf, Rev. George Garner and Hazel Scott were also there to say goodbye to Eddie."

The *Chicago Defender* article stated, in part, "Radio was his forte. He became the lovable Eddie *of Duffy's Tavern* and his quick answers to Ed "Archie" Gardner's problems won him thousands of ardent fans."

The Bloomfield N. J., *Independent Press* printed, "Green, Negro entertainer on *Duffy's Tavern*, died last week in Los Angeles and his many ham (radio) friends mourn his passing. Eddie was a pioneer radio operator receiving his license a mere twenty-five years ago."

The Interment was handled by John Lamar Hill, then President of the Angeles Funeral Home, and the burial took place at the Rosedale Cemetery, on Washington Boulevard in Los Angeles, California.

The relationships that Eddie had with people demonstrated that life is about treating others well, being of service, taking care of business, and sharing your *joie de vivre* with whomever you come across. As well as enjoying good relationships with those around him, Eddie was a loving father. I know, because when I was forty years old, my mother told me that for the first three years of my life, every New Year's Eve, Eddie made it a point to be at my bedside at the stroke of midnight, no matter what. When my mother shared this with me, I actually felt a thump in my chest, like something had poked me and was telling me that Eddie had truly loved me, absolutely. The last lingering resentment I had about Eddie dying when I was still just a young child, vanished.

Eddie became a force in the community. I think he was the type of guy everyone noticed. He was outgoing, funny, and an all-around good guy. He brought laughter and love into people's lives. He was hard-working, as an entertainer and as an entrepreneur. He was a good husband, a good friend, and a good father. Eddie Green was a good man, and, like his song says, "A Good Man is Hard to Find."

Chapter Twenty-Six
Life After Eddie

My mother was not prepared when Eddie died. All she knew was that she had a child, a house, and a car, and no idea what to do with his business affairs. Her part in his life, as his wife, was about looking pretty, being able to cook southern-style meals, traveling, attending parties, clubbing on Central Avenue, and having me (mom told me that she had specifically asked Eddie if he wanted to have a child). Turns out there was no money in the bank. Mom had to borrow money in order to pay for the interment, as well as the hospital and doctor bills. Managing Eddie's business portfolio proved disastrous.

Over the years, as I grew older and began questioning the whereabouts of any documents regarding his studio, his "A Good Man is Hard to Find," or his Masonic affiliation, she would often answer "I don't remember" or "I never asked." She told me that she may have sold the rights to various holdings, but she just could not remember.

Mom had put her opera aspirations on hold while she was married to Eddie, and for whatever reasons, after his death, she chose to leave those aspirations behind. Except for a very short stint on the *Amos 'n' Andy* show in 1951, possibly as a way to have an income, mom never again returned to the entertainment world. In 1952, she sold the house. We moved into an apartment in what is now known as the "Historic West Adams District."

About two years after Eddie died, just before selling the house, mom had been introduced to the brother of one of her friends. His name was Nathaniel (Nate) Beasley. I remember the first time I saw him standing at our front door in his Navy whites. Nate and Norma became a couple, and set up house, in what was then known as "East Los Angeles," on 66th Street.

During this union, mom had four more children, Nathaniel Lance Beasley, Brad Norman Beasley, Donna Marie Beasley, and Brian Beasley. After fifteen years in that union, mom married in 1967 for a third time, to Largett Washington, and remained in that marriage until she passed away in 2010.

Though Norma did not get a chance to see the articles and pictures that I found of her in the newspapers, I console myself that, after all, she was there, and knowing mom, she probably would not have wanted to visit those long past days. I know, however, that she was glad of the fact that I was engaged in the process of writing this book, both as a tribute to my father and as a testament to my grandson.

Thus ends my story of my father's accomplishments as a Black man in the absolute face of obstacles in the early 1900s in America. In the seventeen years of the documentation and writing of this story, I have come to know more about my father than I could ever have imagined. My hope is that by the writing of this book, I will introduce Eddie to those who had no prior knowledge of him, and re-introduce Eddie to those who knew only a little of his works. I have also endeavored to present to my grandson, Edward, a great-grandfather of whom he can be proud, and, perhaps, from whom he can receive inspiration.

Epilogue

Before Eddie died, he saw to it that four of his songs remained in copyright status by renewing the songs. Both "I'm Sorry for It Now" and "I'm Leaving You", were copyrighted on June 21, 1924 and renewed for June 21, 1951.

"The Right Key, But the Wrong Keyhole," with words and melody copyrighted on September 27, 1923, was renewed September 27, 1950.

"Previous," words and music copyrighted December 17, 1923, was renewed December 18, 1950.

Eddie's last movie, *Mr. Adam's Bomb*, was shown a few times after his death, in Philadelphia at The Vogue Theater, along with *Belle of New York* and Sarah Vaughn in *Red Hot Jive*, in 1952. Also, the movie played in 1953 at The Vogue, however, someone made a mistake and listed the title of the movie as, *Mr. Adam's Rib*, featuring Eddie Green, with an all-star colored cast. The movie was shown again on December 16, 1953, at The Vogue, where the newspaper ad announced, "Also Eddie Green, the famous colored comedian in, *Adam's Bomb*."

In 1994, I finally made my way to the Angelus/Rosedale Cemetery on Washington Boulevard to visit my father's grave. After much searching, the lady in the front office realized that she would not be able to tell me exactly where Eddie was buried because, for whatever reason, there was no gravestone. She gave me the name of the man who was supposed to be buried next to Eddie, and said if I found this man, Eddie would be to the right of him. I found Mr. B's headstone, and, sure enough, next to him was smooth ground. I was so upset I walked to the nearest main street, which was Vermont Avenue, and went into a plant store and bought a Ficus plant and a shovel. It was just a six-inch plant, but I needed something to indicate where my father's remains lay.

Due to the sometimes unfortunate circumstances of life, things fall by the wayside, which is what happened in the case of my mother, after Eddie died. She simply did not place a headstone on his grave. Today, what was once a little plant, has become a big tree with roots growing everywhere, a testament to how Eddie's feet were planted on the ground and how he was able to grow and branch out and achieve the heights to which he aspired.

Appendices

List of Songs Written By Eddie Green

1917
Good (A) Man Is Hard to Find; words and music by Eddie Green

1920
Don't Let No One Man Worry Your Mind; words and music by Eddie Green

The Blind Man' Blues, words by Eddie Green, music by Billy McLaurin

Valley (The) of Wonderful Years, words by L. Sears, melody by Eddie Green

You Can't Keep a Good Girl Down; words and melody by Eddie Green, arrangement by H. Qualli Clark

1921
Sun Down, words and music by Eddie Green

World's (The) All Wrong; words by Eddie Green, music by E. Green and Coney Conner

You Can Read My Letters, But You Sure Can't Read My Mind, words and music by Eddie Green

You've Got What I Like; words and music by Eddie Green

1923

King Tut Blues; words and melody by Eddie Green, arrangement by W. Benton Overstreet

Previous, words and music by Eddie Green

Right (The) Key, But the Wrong Keyhole; words and melody by Eddie Green

1924

I'm Leaving You, words and music by Eddie Green

I'm Sorry For It Now, words and music by Eddie Green

1929

Big Business, words and music by Eddie Green

Elinor; words and music by Eddie Green, arrangement by Frederick Watson

Her u-kee-el-a; talking song, words and music by Eddie Green, arrangement by Fred Watson

Kitties (The) Band, talking song, words and music by Eddie Green, music arranged by Fred Watson

Miller (The) o the Glen; talking song, words and music by Eddie Green, music arranged by Fred Watson

Red! Red! Red! talking song, words and music by Eddie Green, arrangement by Fred Watson

She Was a Lovely Girl, talking song, words and music by Eddie Green, arrangement by Fred Watson (words and melody only)

That Didna Trouble Me, talking song, words and music by Eddie Green, music arranged by Fred Watson

U-le-I-o, words and music by Eddie Green, music arranged by Fred Watson

We All Want What We Want When We Want It; written and composed by Eddie Green, music arranged by Fred Watson (words and melody only)

You Never Can Tell, talking song, words and music by Eddie Green, music arranged by Fred Watson (words and melody only)

1932

Find That Darling Baby, words by Frank Ceinta and W. A. Wright, and music by Morton Levine and Eddie Green; pf, treble

List of Movies Written, Directed, and Produced By Eddie Green
Starring Eddie Green

Sepia Art Pictures Corporation
1939

Dress Rehearsal,

What Goes Up,

1940

Comes Midnight,

1941

One Round Jones,

Sepia Productions, Incorporated
1949

Mr. Adam's Bomb

List of Movies in Which Eddie Green Appeared

1929 Vitaphone

Sending a Wire

1930 Vitaphone

Crap Game

Temple Bells

Devil's Parade

1938 Warner Bros.

Boarder Trouble

1945 Paramount

Ed Gardner's Duffy's Tavern

1946

Mantan Messes Up

List of *Jubilee* Appearances in the Book

December 25, 1942:

Count Basie, Delta Rhythm Boys, Lena Horne, Bing Crosby, and Ernest Whitman. Ernest and Eddie perform "Christmas Present"

January 15, 1943

Jimmy Lunceford, Maxine Sullivan, Charioteers, and Canada Lee. Canada Lee and Eddie perform "Boxing"

May, 1944:
Bob Parish, Dorothy Donnegan and the Sweethearts of Rhythm. Ernest Whitman and Eddie perform a sketch regarding Eddie getting a job.

October, 1944
Erskine Hawkins, Effie Smith, Eddie South, Jimmy Mitchell, Leadbelly, and Ernest Whitman. Ernest and Eddie perform "Volunteer Fireman"

July, 1945
Count Basie Orchestra, Ann Moore, Hattie McDaniel, Ernest Whitman. Hattie and Eddie perform "Napoleon and Josephine"

List of *Duffy's Tavern* Skits in the Book
January 5, 1943
New Year's Resolution

January 5, 1945
Archie Quits

January 12, 1945
Young Monster Malone

November 9, 1945
Eddie Quits

December 18, 1946
Sonia Jones

November 5, 1947
Testimonial dinner for Archie, given by Archie

April 20, 1949
Cass Daley sings "A Good Man Is Hard to Find"

May 30, 1950
Tony Martin

List of *Amos 'n' Andy* Sketches in the Book
March 25, 1947
Broken Down Trailer

May 20, 1947
The Alligator Bag

October 10, 1948
Lulu Mae Simpson Is Coming to Town

December 26, 1948
Sapphire Leaves

List of Radio Shows in Which Eddie Green Appeared
1934
The General Tire Review

The Royal Desserts Hour

1936
Fleischman's Yeast Hour

Rudy Vallee

1937

The Royal Gelatin Hour

Rudy Vallee

1938

The Royal Desserts Hour

1939

The Pursuit of Happiness

1940

Forecast

Rudy Vallee

The Jell-O Program

The Pursuit of Happiness

1941

The Columbia Workshop

The Jell-O Program

1942

Stage Door Canteen

The Columbia Workshop

1943

Meet the Colonel

1944

Mail Call

Radio Hall of Fame

1945

Radio Hall of Fame

To the Rear March

1946-47

Beulah

Caravan

The Fabulous Dr. Tweedy

The Folks on Fourth Street

To the Rear March

1948

Mirth and Melody

Index

Made in the USA
Middletown, DE
11 August 2018